Excel Can Talk?

ONE KEYSTROKE CHARTS?

EXCEL IS FEMALE?

50+ SECRETS OF
MICROSOFT EXCEL® 2013
YOU WOULD HAVE NEVER THOUGHT
OF GOOGLING

Sofia Santiago, MBA, PMP

Excel Can Talk? One Keystroke Charts?
Excel 2013 Is Female?
50+ Features of Microsoft Excel 2013® You Would Have
Naver Thought of Googling
By Sofia Santiago, MBA, PMP
Cover design by Dani De la Chica

ISBN-13: 978-1523412884

ISBN-10: 1523412887

Sofia Santiago, MBA. PMP

Lee's Summit, Missouri.

For information on volume discounts, bulk orders, and/or workshops please contact us through
www.ExcelCanTalk.com

It's true hard work
never killed anybody,
but I figure,
why take the chance?

—Ronald Reagan

Contents

Yes! 5

   Secret #1. Excel® Is a Woman 5

   Secret #2. She Can Talk 8

   Secret#3. She Reads Your Data out Loud as
              You Enter It... 13

   Secret #4. Word® Can Talk Too 13

   Secret #5. One Keystroke Charts............................. 14

   There You Have It 20

Secrets That Not Even Advanced Users Know 20

   Secret #6. How to Keep Your Favorite Stuff in a
              Handy Place 20

   Secret #7. How to Add to Your Sheets All the
              Power of Word ® 29

   Secret #8. How to Create a "Favorites" List of
              Workbooks 34

   Secret #9. How to Keep Your Stuff Secret by
              "Very-Hiding" It 37

   Secret #10. How Have You Lived Not Knowing
              About Ctrl + G ? 43

   Secret #11. How to Find or Extract Unique
              Values 44

Shortcuts That Deal With Multiple Items at Once 46

   Secret #12. Multiple Selection Shortcuts 46

   Secret #13. Multiple Autosum 49

   Secret #14. Viewing Multiple Sheets At Once 52

Secret #15. Opening Multiple Files at Once 56

Secret #16. Multiple Copy-Pastes 57

Secret #17. Multiple Undos 61

Shortcuts to Enter Data Way Faster 63

Secret #18. How to Save a Lot of Clicks When
Entering Data.. 63

Secret #19. How to Enter Data into Multiple
Cells at Once 65

Secret #20. How to Create a Drop-Down List.............. 67

Secret #21. How to Repeat the Previous Row's
Entry 70

Secret #22. How to Create a Spin Button 71

Secret #23. Enter Zip Codes, Phones, or SSNs
Fast 76

Secret #24. How to Enter Data Through a
Cool-Beans Form.. 77

The Black Little Square 81

Basic Concepts 81

Secret #25. Double Click the Thingy.......................... 85

Secret #26. Create Sequences or Patterns 87

Secret #27. List Only Weekdays................................. 90

Secret #28. Right Click-Thingying 92

Secret #29. Shift-Thingying 93

Secret #30. Ctrl-Thingying.. 95

Secret #31. Create a List and Sort by It..................... 96

Secret #32. Autofill Sparklines 102

Secret #33. How to use Flash Fill ("FiFi") to
Split Texts 106

Secret #34. How to use FiFi to Change the Case
of Text 110

Best Places to Double Click 111

Secret #35. On Any Dialog Box to Skip the OK......... 111

Secret #36. A Ribbon Tab's Edge 112

Secret #37. A Row's or a Column's Edge 113

Secret #38. A Sheet Tab 114

Secret #39. The Format Painter Tool 114

Secret #40. The Autosum Icon................................ 116

Secret #41. A Formula.. 118

Secret #42. A Chart... 119

Secret #43. On a Cell's Border................................ 120

The Most Powerful Keyboard Shortcuts 121

Secret #44. How to Execute Any Command
with Your Keyboard............................... 121

Secret #45. Don't Lose Ctrl + 1 124

Secret #46. Ctrl + Mustache 127

Secret #47. How to Split the Text Inside One
Cell Into Two or More Lines.................... 130

Secret #48. Cloning Sheets Without Even Right
Clicking! 131

Secret #49. Shift Happens®..................................... 134

Secret #50. Moving in a New York Minute 136

Epilogue 141

Acknowledgments 143

Works Cited...144

Yes!

Yes, Excel® can talk.

Yes, you can create a chart with just one click.

And yes, Excel is female.

Let's start by addressing this last question, because once you understand this fundamental fact of life, many of the questions you've had about Excel® will be automatically answered.

Secret #1. Excel® Is a Woman

The proof has been there all along, but in case you haven't been paying attention, here's a list of reasons that prove Excel® is female:

- She is incredibly smart.

- She can do *anything* (as long as you know how to ask her *nicely*.)

- She points out your errors and even offers to fix them[1].

- She tries to complete your sentences before you do[2].

---

[1] As long as the background error checking feature is enabled (*File* ⇨ *Options* ⇨ *Formulas* ⇨ *Error Checking* ⇨ *Enable background error checking*).

[2] *Autocomplete* and *Autocorrect* are two features related to this ability. Have you noticed that when you start entering text into a cell Excel® tries to guess the whole word before you type it? Sure, this only

- She's spectacular at remembering dates. Actually, she remembers *everything* you've done[3].

- The more you discover all her talents, the more you realize how awesome she is.

- The older she gets, the nicer and wiser she is[4].

- Some people think that Excel® is hard to understand, erratic, unpredictable, or maybe even "difficult"? Some others have even felt that they have a love-hate relationship with their Excel®. Well, the truth is exactly the opposite: she is *very* logical and she *always* does the right thing (mostly). If someone doubts it, all it means is that he hasn't devoted enough time and

---

happens when you've typed other text that starts with the same characters, which is the one Excel guesses you want to type again. This is the *Autocomplete* feature. *Autocorrect* is the feature that allows Excel® to automatically correct typos and misspelled words.

[3] Zak (2012). When discussing the differences between male's and female's brains, university professor and neuroeconomist Paul Zak, Ph. D. explains that the hippocampus, which generates long term memory, is bigger in women and that's why they remember things better. As for Excel®, read Secret #17 to learn about how she remembers the last 100 tasks you've performed, and how that can benefit *you.*

[4] Those of you who started using Excel® 30 years ago may remember that she was not as *intuitive, user-friendly,* or *customizable* as she is now. She didn't predict your actions as accurately as she does now, and she didn't know how to do many of the things she knows how to do now (such as flash fill, pivottable reports, conditional formatting, data validation, drop down lists, etc.)

energy to fully understand her (so it's their fault, *obviously*.)

- She's overworked and underappreciated[5].

- She's a mind reader. Some say that it is *intuition*, and some others say that it is pattern recognition and extrapolation. Either way, that's *female* my friend! Here's how it works: She uses pattern recognition to extract and/or to concatenate data, and then she extrapolates (that's how she knows what you'll likely want to do next[6].) For instance, let's say that a guy has been staying at work late. She takes notice (pattern recognition). She knows his office just hired a new receptionist that used to be a Victoria Secret® model in her native Brazil (because he mentioned it and she would never forget it. Remember she's female?) She puts two and two together (sums or concatenates data), and with that she extrapolates: she knows what he'd like to do next (are you with me?)

"Oh," you may be thinking... "That makes sense."

Right.

---

5   A lot of people think so (mostly women).

6   I'm not kidding... this is how Excel's *Flash Fill* feature works. Secrets #33 and #34 will tell you what Flash Fill can do for you.

Secret #2. She Can Talk

Try this with me.

1	Fire up your Excel®
2	Your choice: (a) in a new sheet type the data illustrated below[7], or (b) open any of the boring worksheets you usually work with[8].

	A	B
1	The five highest-paying jobs that you can get with a high school degree	
2		
3	Job	High-End Annual Income
4	Gaming manager at a casino	$116,000
5	Ship captain	$117,000
6	Detective	$119,000
7	Elevator installer	$101,000
8	Web developer	$119,000

3	Now we will add a new command to your *Quick Access Toolbar (QAT)* and then we'll use it.

---

[7] Aol (2011).

[8] If you're feeling adventurous today try this: when typing the numbers, type a dollar symbol and then the number. Don't type the commas; Excel® inserts them automatically. Go ahead, it's okay. It's okay to type the $ so you won't need to format the numbers later. See? You're already learning tricks ☺. Oh, and if you don't know how to make the title look this cool (centered over several columns and split into several lines) don't worry. You'll learn how to do it later in this book (Check out Secret #47.)

Find the *Quick Access Toolbar* (it's the line of icons that contains little images that represent the *Save*, *Undo*, and *Redo* commands. It will likely be in the top left corner of your screen)[9]:

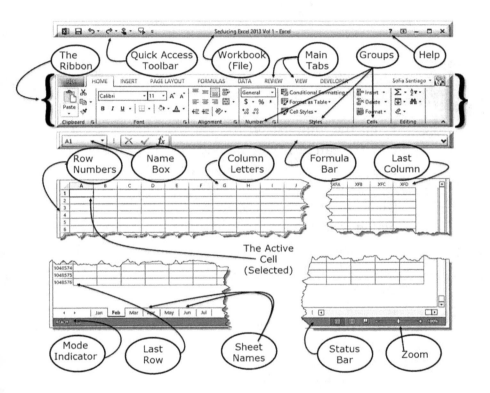

9 "I don't know where it is because I've never needed to use the *Undo* command" is one of those big fat lies that no one believes, so don't even try. It's worse than "She's only a friend," or "It's not the money, it's the principle." Geez! It's even worse than "Open wide, it won't hurt a bit!" (Have you ever seen a dentist?)

4 Click on the down arrow (shown right below this text) and select *More Commands*. The *Customize the QAT* dialog box opens up. See illustration on the next page.

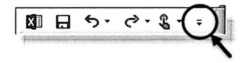

5 In the *Choose commands from* drop-down list (top left) select *Commands not in The Ribbon*.

6 From the long list on the left side, select *Speak cells*[10] (I can hear you already thinking something like "Get outta here!" or "OMG!")

7 Click on the *Add* button in the middle of the dialog box. You just added the *Speak cells* command to your *QAT*, so you can see it on the right side immediately after the *Undo* and *Redo* commands.

8 Lets' test drive it. Click on any cell that contains data.

9 Click on the icon for the *Speak cells* command in the *QAT*.

---

[10] Scroll all the way down to it, or click on any command, then type "S" to jump to the first command that starts with that letter, and then scroll the last part of the way.

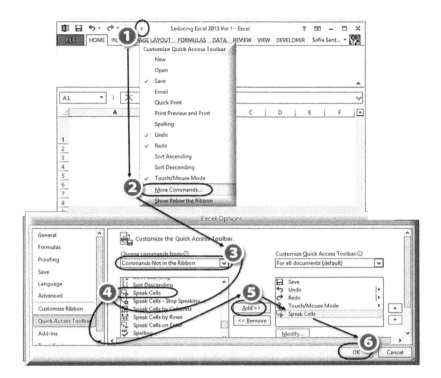

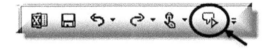

Yes, Excel® is reading your information out loud!

Plop? Did I just hear you faint?

Now, joking aside, do you see the practical application of this feature? Yes? Okay, tell me. No, no, no, you go first. Me? Fine. Well, here's one I can think of: after you copy data from a source paper document, and you need to make sure you made no mistakes, have Excel® read the figures back to you. Great way to proofread! I know you've been using your favorite coworker to help you with that, but from now you can have Excel® be your personal assistant.

Can You Make Her Stop?

We are going to repeat steps 8 and 9 from page 10, so we can make Excel® speak again. Only this time before you click on *Speak cells,* get ready to pause her (yes, Excel® silly, who else?) in the middle of her reading .... After she reads a few, press *Esc* and you'll see how she stops. After a few seconds, click on the *Speak cells* command again and watch how she resumes her reading from where she left off.

Is that awesome or what!? HA! [11]

Now are you thinking that perhaps Excel® should be your new BFF? Well, maybe... How many of your girlfriends have ever had a "Shhh!" (Shut up) button you can press when you need a break from their talking? Didn't think so. How many of your girlfriends would *not* have their feelings hurt because you interrupted them so harshly? Didn't think so either[12].

Oh, by the way, instead of using the Esc key, you can add the *Speak Cells – Stop Speaking Cells* command to your Quick Access Toolbar using Secret #6.

One Last Note

I know the question that's been bugging you since several pages ago. Don't worry, I won't leave it unanswered. Here's the answer: No.

---

[11] If Excel®'s voice sounds.... Mmhh.... kind of manly, perhaps she has laryngitis. Oh well. She'll get well someday.

[12] It's not a "Mute" button. She actually stops talking so you can resume later without having missed a bit.

No, sorry, you can't change Excel®'s voice so she will sound like George Clooney. Believe me, I've tried. Something you can do, though, is change the speed at which she speaks (and maybe even change her voice). This is something that people who type really fast and use the *Speak Cells on Enter* (just explained) will appreciate. For details contact me through www.SofiaSantiago.com or www.CanExcelTalk.com.

Secret #3. She Reads Your Data out Loud as You Enter It

In the same place where you found the *Speak Cells* command, a few rows below it, you'll find *Speak Cells on Enter*. That's another great command to add to your QAT. It works like a light switch: you turn it on by clicking on it, and when you no longer need it you click again on it to turn it off. When it's on, Excel® will read back to you whatever you type into a cell as soon as you hit *Enter*.

If you can type without looking at your keyboard, this feature will give you instant feedback. Can you see how you can use this to catch any typing errors on the spot and save time?

Secret #4. Word® Can Talk Too

You can also have Word® read your documents out loud. The process to customize the Quick Access Toolbar in Word® is exactly the same as in Excel®: just follow steps 3 to 7 on pages 8, 9 and 10 inside of Word® (or read Secret #6.) The only difference is that in Word® the command is *Speak*, not *Speak*

Cells. I'm sure you can figure out why without needing to hire Sherlock Holmes.

Secret #5. One Keystroke Charts

Use method #1 (keyboard shortcuts) if:

- You are the type of person that likes to make his or her own decisions... street smart... a self-made cookie... or

- You sometimes use Excel® 2013 but some others use an older version (2010 or 2007), or you give support to others who do, and want to know a method that works for all of those versions, or

- You were born between 1946 and 1964 (and therefore you're a workaholic baby-boomer), or

- You have a hard time delegating. You get a kick out of micro-managing others (including Excel®).

Use method #2 (the Quick Analysis Tool) if:

- You are the emotionally-intelligent kind of guy or girl... you know, the kind that's in touch with their feminine side... or

- You already know how awesome Excel® is and you're willing to put your destiny in her hands and let her recommend what's best for you, or

- You are great at delegating (or pretty lazy, yeah.)

Method #1: Keyboard Shortcuts

1   Select the data you want to chart. If you only have a list of labels (like months) and a number to the right of each one, you don't need to select the whole area. Just click on any one of the cells in that range. Excel® is smart enough to understand which data you want to chart.

2   To create the chart in a new sheet press *F11*. To create it in the active sheet press *Alt + F1*.

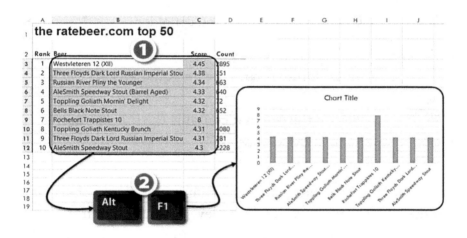

Excel® creates a column chart, which is the most common type. You can edit it any way you want, for instance changing its title.

A Dynamic Chart Title

You may have noticed in the previous illustration that the title reads "Chart Title." Blagh. Does that make you feel some anxiety? It certainly makes me, and I'm sure I'm not the only obsessive compulsive around here... Oh, well. If you want to deny it that's fine with me. Let's fix the title anyway.

Click on the text box that's the placeholder for the title. Once it's selected you can edit it by (a) typing a title right there in-situ, or (b) by typing the title in the formula bar.

Since many times you'll want your chart title to be the same as your data title, here's a trick you'll like:

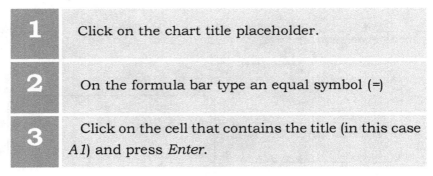

1	Click on the chart title placeholder.
2	On the formula bar type an equal symbol (=)
3	Click on the cell that contains the title (in this case *A1*) and press *Enter*.

Did you like that? By using a formula for the chart title rather than a constant text, whenever you change the title for your data the chart's title will be automatically updated. Ta da!

Column Chart or Bar Chart?

I'd like to change the chart to a bar type, just because the categories (beers) are too long. Ahh.... Much better. I like my beers better in a bar.

To do so I activated the chart (by clicking on its frame) and then I issued the command *Chart Tools* ⇨ *Design* ⇨ *Change Chart Type* ⇨ *Bar*. Explore the different subtypes illustrated in the top row of this dialog box, and hover over the chart illustrations to magnify them slightly and choose better.

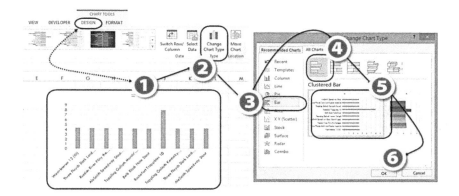

The "categories" are the words that label each column, along the horizontal axis. When they are too long, it's a best practice to use a bar chart (horizontal bars) rather than a column chart (vertical bars). This, in a nutshell, is the difference between those two types of charts. You can use it as a guideline to decide which one to use.

Actually, there is a second instance when a horizontal bar chart will do a better job than a column chart: it is when you have so many categories that fitting all the columns required for all categories would make the chart look too busy.

More Charting Best Practices

Here are a few more best practices:

- When the categories represent time (for instance months[13]), use a line chart rather than a column chart.

- Be careful when using 3D charts. When you need accuracy avoid them. This is the one area where I've found that she is not perfect.

- To illustrate which percentage of a total each element represents, use a pie. Keep it to less than 7 slices though, or it will look busy.

- Before you create a chart, ask yourself, "What's the one message I want my audience to immediately understand when they see this chart?" Only one message per chart. If you have more than one message, create more than one chart.

- Avoid using the advanced chart types (radar, bubbles, surface, and stock) unless you are absolutely sure your audience will know how to interpret them (or you'll take the time to teach them.) You don't want to make them feel stupid if they don't understand.

Method #2: With the Quick Analysis Tool

1	Select the data you want to chart.
2	The *Quick Analysis Button* pops up near the bottom right corner of the selection. Click on it.

---

[13] Did I really need to include that example?

3   Select *Charts*.

4   Excel® shows you a list of recommended charts followed by the *More Charts* icon. Hover over any chart to see it magnified. If you like any of them pick it and you're done.

5   If you don't like any of the recommended charts (or you are just a contrarian by nature) click on *More*. In the *Insert Chart* dialog box select the second tab: *All Charts*. Pick the chart type (leftmost column) you want, the sub-type (top row), and then the specific chart (center).

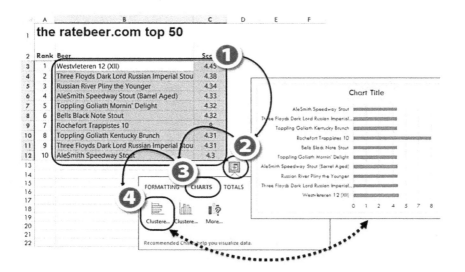

There You Have It

Now you know the answers to the questions on the cover. Now be honest, would you have thought of googling any of them? If so, wow! Are you a guy and are you single? I only ask because it seems you have a lot of time on your hands… Or is it that you googled, "Is there any command that I don't know about?" Either way, keep reading to see how many of the remaining 45 secrets you would have thought of googling.

Secrets That Not Even Advanced Users Know[14]

Secret #6. How to Keep Your Favorite Stuff in a Handy Place

What percentage of Excel®'s commands do you use on a regular basis? Would you say that 50%? 10%? Nah. More like 1%? "Dunno but not a lot"? Okay —that's a more statistically accurate answer, good. So how about, instead of having to click-click-click all day long all over different tabs to find the

---

[14] If you already knew all of them then you're not an advanced user: you're a guru. Tell your coworkers to start bowing down when you come in every day.

commands you use, we place them in a handy place, so we can have them easily accessible? That's what the *Quick Access Toolbar (QAT)* is for. Do the words "quick access" ring a bell?

How may knowing this help you? Well, here are some ideas:

' If you tend to loose stuff (keys, glasses, commands...) you'll want to place them all in the same handy place so you won't waste time trying to find them every time[15].

' If you just migrated to a new version of Excel® and haven't memorized yet where each command is, why not place the ones you use most on the QAT? (Use Method #2 explained ahead.)

' If you need to get help working on your sheets from someone who's not proficient at using Excel®, why not place the commands they'll use on the QAT, so you'll train them faster only in what they'll use?

' If you want to use *Commands not in The Ribbon* (such as the *Speak cells* command you need a place to put them so you can click on them. This place can be the QAT.

• Your sweetie's b-day is approaching fast and you haven't had time to get her that $20K turquoise leather Hermes® handbag, or the $4K Jimmy Choo's shoes she asked you for? No problem! Why not customize her QAT instead? What a unique gift she'll never forget![16]

---

[15] I *know* I'm not your mom – just trying to help here.

[16] She'll tell everyone about it. Trust me.

To Show the QAT Below *The Ribbon*

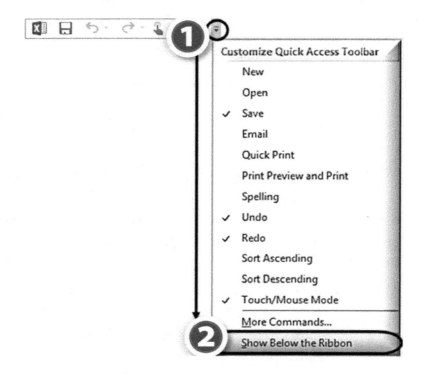

1	Click on the QAT's drop down arrow.
2	Select the last option: *Show Below The Ribbon*. This is the first thing you'll want to do, just because it does make sense to have your favorite commands as close to your spreadsheet as possible.

Because most of the time you'll be working somewhere on the grid, you can cumulatively save hours by moving your mouse a shorter distance every time you need to click on a command. Even if your ribbon is only one inch tall, hey, one inch is one inch, right? Ask anybody and they'll agree that it does make a difference.

To Add Popular Commands to Your QAT

1	Click on the QAT's drop down arrow.
2	Click on the command you want to add so that it's checked.

This is a limited method that allows you to add only commands from that list. Still, it's handy to add exactly what it says: popular commands.

To Add Your Favorite Commands from *The Ribbon* (Method #1)

1	Right click on your favorite command.
2	Select Add to QAT.

Some commands include a drop down arrow to their right. If you right click on the command you'll add that command only, whereas if you right click on the arrow you'll add all the other options you have access to when you click on that arrow.

As an example, if you click on the word *Autosum* (*Editing* group on the right side of the *Home* tab) to add the sum function you'll only be adding that function. If, instead, you click on the drop-down arrow to the right of the word *Autosum,* you'll be adding to your QAT all the other statistical functions (Average, Count numbers, Max, Min, etc.) Excel® makes available to you[17].

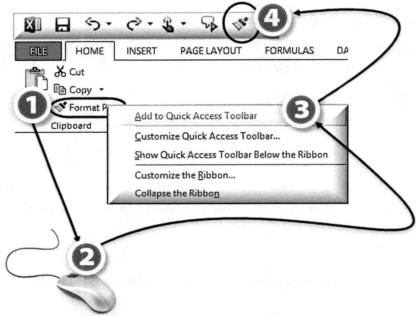

To Add Your Favorite Commands from *The Ribbon* (Method #2)

---

[17] Remember to exercise caution when using statistical functions, because statistics are Excel®'s bikini: even when what they show is attention-grabbing, the best part is likely hidden.

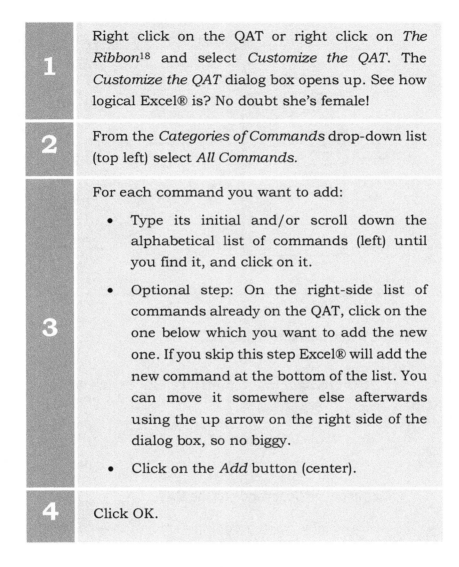

1 Right click on the QAT or right click on *The Ribbon*[18] and select *Customize the QAT*. The *Customize the QAT* dialog box opens up. See how logical Excel® is? No doubt she's female!

2 From the *Categories of Commands* drop-down list (top left) select *All Commands*.

3 For each command you want to add:

- Type its initial and/or scroll down the alphabetical list of commands (left) until you find it, and click on it.

- Optional step: On the right-side list of commands already on the QAT, click on the one below which you want to add the new one. If you skip this step Excel® will add the new command at the bottom of the list. You can move it somewhere else afterwards using the up arrow on the right side of the dialog box, so no biggy.

- Click on the *Add* button (center).

4 Click OK.

---

[18] You can also select *File* ⇨ *Options* ⇨ *Quick Access Toolbar* or click on the down arrow that's all the way to the right of the QAT and select *More Commands*.

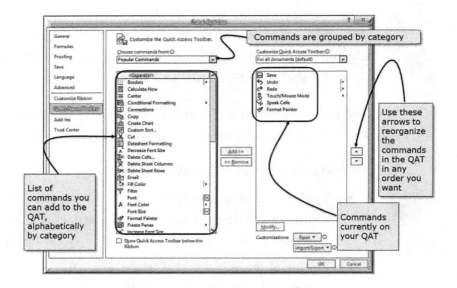

To Remove a Command from the QAT

1	Right click on the command's icon on the QAT.
2	Select *Remove* from QAT.

To Rearrange the Commands on the QAT

If you frantically started adding commands because you were so excited you couldn't wait any longer good for you. Love that passion! On the other hand, chances are you added them in a random order, and therefore your QAT probably looks like a total mess at this point. Not to worry – we'll fix that. No, you don't need to remove them and start all over.

1 Open the QAT customization box. Observe it[19].

2 Do you see the up and down arrow all the way to the right, close to the vertical middle of the dialog box? Good job. You use those to change the order of the commands in your QAT:

- Select the command you want to move.

- Click the arrow button that points in the direction you want to move it.

How to Add Separators to Group Commands

Separators are the little vertical lines (pipes) that delimit groups of commands.

It's a good idea to add many to group commands in an organized manner – why not, they are free!

1 Click on the down arrow to the right of the QAT. Select *More Commands*. The *Customize the QAT* dialog box opens up. On the left side you can see all the commands organized by categories.

---

[19] Observe it on your computer screen or look at the illustration above. If you're not close to your computer, you'll want to pick the second option. You'll also want to pick the second option if you're driving a car while reading this.

| 2 | Pick any category and scroll all the way to the top of the list of commands. The first option will be *<Separator>*. Click on *<Separator>*. |
| 3 | Add it and/or move it up or down as you would any command. |

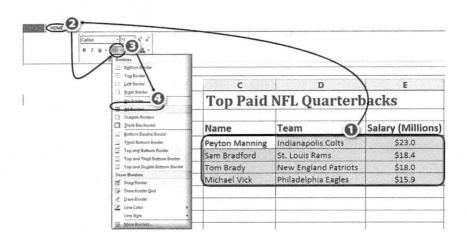

Example

Let's assume for just a sec that you're obsessive compulsive, and you go nuts if you don't add borders (all four sides of them) to your cells. This means that what you've likely been doing so far, over and over, is:

1. Selecting the cells you want to place borders around.

2. Clicking on *Home* ⇨ *Borders* drop down arrow ⇨ *All Borders* (this is the two by two little grid).

Now you want to add the *All Borders* command to your QAT. This is what you'll do:

- Make the *All Borders* command visible. To do this, you may need to apply it to any random cell (by following steps 1 and 2 above).

- Right click on the *All Borders* command icon and select *Add to Quick Access Toolbar.*

- Now click the *Undo* command to remove the border you added to that random cell[20].

Secret #7. How to Add to Your Sheets All the Power of *Word* ®

Sometimes you want to include memos, letters, instructions, rules, or other long texts in your spreadsheets, and Excel®'s text boxes are too limited in terms of their formatting capabilities. Word® is much more powerful when it comes to managing texts, so why not bring her over?

---

[20] Unless you want to keep it as a souvenir of this chapter, hehe.

Actually, the *Undo* command worked here, but there'll be other times when you want to remove formatting, but since that was not the latest action you performed, the *Undo* command won't do it. Here's an easy way to remove the formatting from cells: in the *Home* tab, there's a group of commands called *Editing*. Do you see the icon of an eraser on the bottom left side of that group? Right click on it and add it to your QAT. In the future, when you want to remove the formatting from any cell(s), all you'll need to do is select them, click on the eraser, and tell Excel® to clear the format, the contents, or both.

1	Select the top left corner of the range where you want the text (you'll be able to move it later if you want to, so don't worry about precision.)
2	Select *Insert* ⇨ *Object* ⇨ *Word Document*. The *Create New Tab* is selected by default.
3	Click *OK*.
4	Type your document in the new box. Notice that Excel®'s Ribbon has been replaced by Word®'s Ribbon, so you can use any of Word®'s features.
5	Click *OK*.
6	When you're done click outside of the document frame. You can move it or resize it[21].
7	To go back into the document to edit it double click inside the box[22].
8	To eliminate or change the border select the frame (get out of the box first by clicking outside of it, then click on its frame), and then go to

---

[21] Just like you would any other object. Clicking on its frame to "activate it", and then clicking on a corner and dragging it (to resize it), or clicking on any of its sides and dragging it (to move it).

[22] Think about the changes *before* double clicking inside the book (you don't want people to think that you are an "inside-the-box-thinker.")

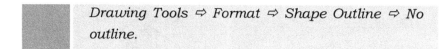

Drawing Tools ⇨ Format ⇨ Shape Outline ⇨ No outline.

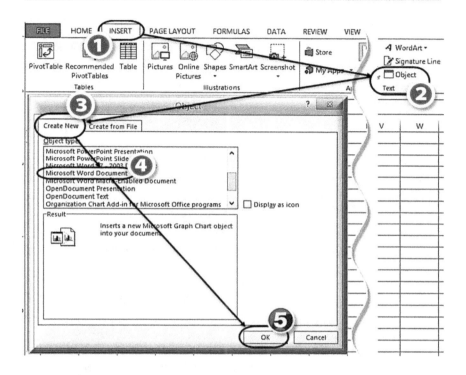

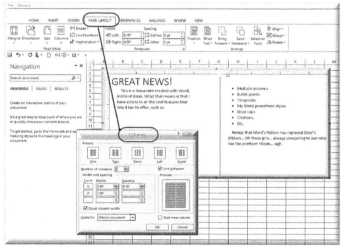

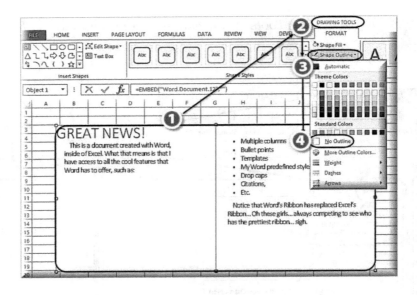

Embedding Documents, pdfs, PowerPoint® Presentations, etc.

You can use a similar process to insert existing Word® documents into your worksheets, did you notice? The nerdy term is *to embed them.*

Why? Well, maybe to keep them all in the same place, or to email or store this file with all the "attachments" or additional documents it refers to, regardless of the software used to create them.

For instance, imagine you're working on evaluating potential external consultants to work with you on a certain project. You've created a comparison worksheet, and you want to keep all the information about each of the consultants that are competing to work with you centralized in just one file. In that comparison table each row has information about one consultant: the company name, the rep's name, title, his or her phone numbers, etc. You could add a column titled 'Bid' and for each row embed a Word® file with the scanned file of the quote they've submitted.

Moreover, when embedding those files, you could elect to show them only as icons rather than as the open documents. That way, whenever you wanted to open any of them, you could just double click on the icon.

I'm sure you could come up with other good reasons for Excel® to agree on having her girlfriend Word® stay over. Or her girlfriend Adobe® the Acrobat®.

Here's something absolutely, totally awesome about embedding other files into your spreadsheets. Look at the illustration that shows the process:

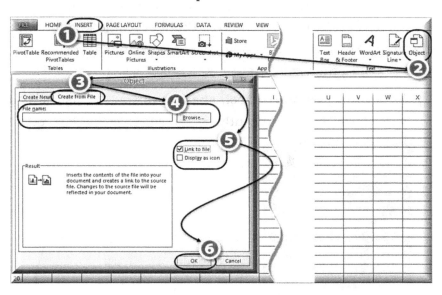

Notice the check box to the left of *Link to File*. Got it? Guess what happens when you click to place a checkmark there before clicking OK.... Yup. Excel® creates a link, so whenever you make changes to the Word® file (or to any other type of source file), the embedded image reflects the changes immediately in your Excel® worksheet. Is that cool or what?

Secret #8. How to Create a "Favorites" List of Workbooks

If you ever used Excel 2010, do you remember the *File* ⇨ *Recent* command? Yeah, the one that showed you the list of books you had recently worked with, so you could click on any of them to open it back up instead of having to navigate your folders like crazy trying to find it. You didn't? You don't? Oh, well... No problem. In Excel 2013 that command is gone with the wind. No need to cry though, since now finding your recent files is easier than ever! Here's how this works now:

1) When you just start Excel, she shows you the list of files you've worked with recently on the left side of the screen:

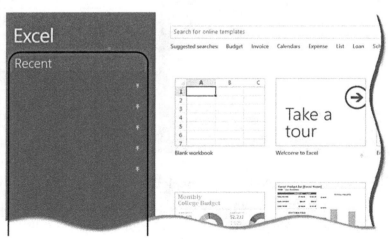

2) When you click on the *File* tab, you go to what Microsoft calls *"the backstage view"*.... Ooh.... Doesn't that sound

exciting? Mysterious? Yeah, I know, like a place where only VIPs are allowed, right? Well, on the left side of the screen, where you go "backstage" you can see your favorite(s) and/or your recent file(s)

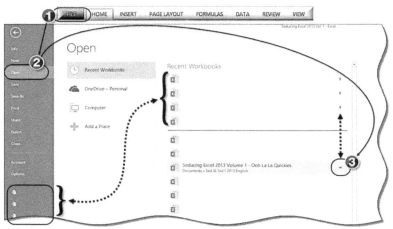

3) When you go to *File* ⇨ *Open* Excel shows you (on the right side, as illustrated above) the list of *Recent Workbooks*, have you noticed?

Well, something that not everyone knows is that you can click on the gray pin to the right of any file name to permanently pin it to the recent files list. That way, it will never go away from the list, until you directly kick it to the curb (by clicking on its pin again). After you've "pinned" at least one file, the list seems to be divided into two lists (separated by a horizontal line): the upper one has the "pinned" files, which are your favorites that won't go away, in alphabetical order; the lower list is the rolling list of recent files.

You can tell Excel how many files you want to keep in your recent file list by going to *File* ⇨ *Advanced* ⇨ *Display* ⇨ *Show this number of recent workbooks* (up to 50).

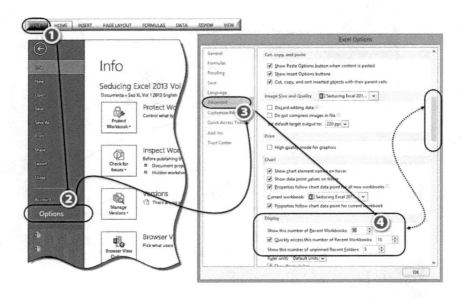

Secret #9. How to Keep Your Stuff Secret by "Very-Hiding" It

Let's recap the three options you may already know to hide info:

1. Hiding rows or columns
2. Hiding the cells that contain the formulas
3. Hiding the whole sheet

Hiding Rows or Columns

You can hide rows or columns by Selecting them ⇨ right clicking ⇨ *Hide.*

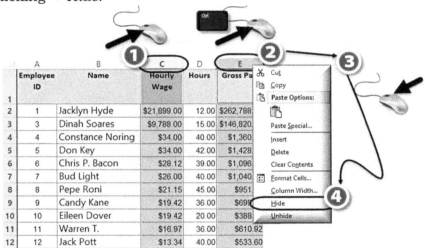

See Secret #12 for a refresher on selecting areas. In the illustration I used the Ctrl key to select two non-contiguous columns.

Hiding Formulas

You can let others see the results of your formulas, but hide the formulas themselves by *Selecting* them ⇨ *Right Click* ⇨ *Format Cells* ⇨ *Protection* tab ⇨ Check *Hidden* ⇨ *OK*. This won't take effect until you enable protection: *Review* Tab ⇨ *Protect Sheet* ⇨ *OK*.

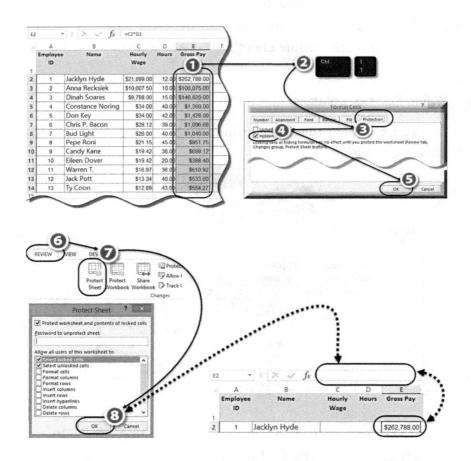

Notice that when the cells with hidden formulas are selected, the formula bar shows nothing (left), and Ctrl + Mustache[23] (the *Show Formulas* shortcut) doesn't show them either:

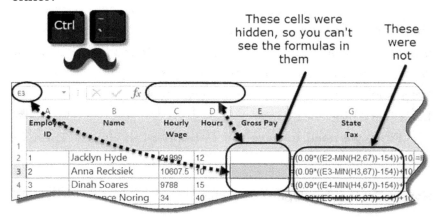

Hiding the Whole Enchilada

You can hide the whole sheet, right? Right click on the sheet name ⇨ *Hide.*

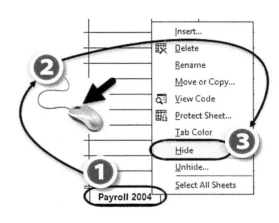

---

[23] This is Shortcut #6.3.

But The Problem Is...

Now here's the thing: many users already know all those commands, so they can easily "reverse" them to find your stuff. For instance, if they right click on any sheet name, and there are other hidden sheets, the *Unhide* command is not grayed out (yeah, Excel® gives you away, oops!) so they know right there you're hiding something, sneaky nerd! Really?? Let's show them how sneaky and nerdy we can be, shall we? Let's "very hide" our junk!

First, we need to have the *Developer* tab visible. Then we will "very-hide" your sheet.

How to Get the *Developer* Tab Visible

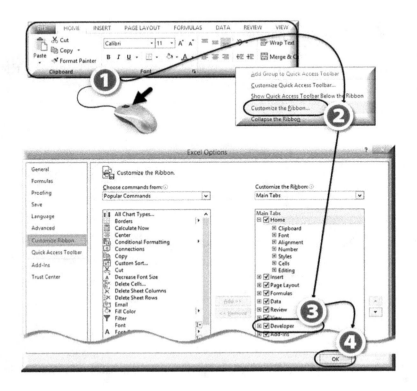

1   Right click anywhere on The Ribbon and select *Customize The Ribbon.*

2   On the right side there's a list of the main tabs, groups and commands currently visible on The Ribbon. It's an outline, and the first level includes the names of the main tabs: *Home, Insert, Page Layout,* etc. In that list find *Developer.* Make sure it's checked (Yes, if you uncheck a tab and then click OK, it will not be visible. Do not do that to your coworkers: don't hide their tabs!)

3   Click OK.

Change the Visibility Property for the Sheet

1   Open up the visual basic window: *Developer* ➪ *Visual Basic* (in the *Code* group.)

2   If the *Properties* window is not already open, press *F4* to open it up (see the illustration on the next page.)

3   If the *Project Explorer* window is not already open, press *Ctrl + R* to open it up. This window shows each open workbook as a *VBAProject,* and just below its name, a folder that contains all the *Microsoft Excel Objects* in that workbook, including all the sheets in it.

4	In the *Project Explorer* select the sheet you want to "very hide."
5	In the *Properties* Window scroll down to the last property, (*Visibility*). Click on its value (*xlSheetvisible*) and a drop down opens up.
6	Pick the last option: *2 – SheetVeryHidden*.
7	To go back to your sheet, close the *Project Explorer* window (click the top right corner X) or click on the Excel® icon (left). You can't see the "very hidden" sheet anywhere. Ha!

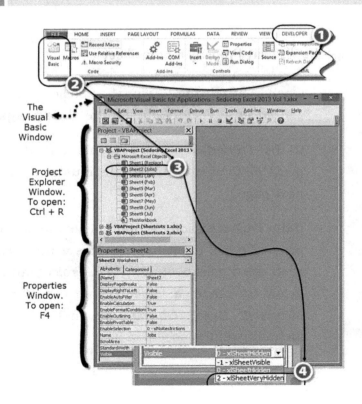

Secret #10. How Have You Lived Not Knowing About Ctrl + G ?

1	Bring up the *Go To Special* dialog box by: (a) Pressing *F5* and then clicking on *Special,* or (b) Pressing *Ctrl + G* and clicking *Special, or* (c) Doing *Home ⇨ Find & Select (Editing group) ⇨ Go To Special.*
2	Select the type of cells you want to find, such as blanks, formulas, cells that have validation rules, or conditional formatting, etc.
3	Click *OK.* Excel® selects those cells in the active sheet. Now you can format them, or lock them, or process them any way you want[24].

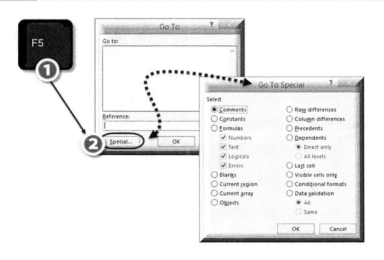

---

[24] The example for Secret #19 also illustrates the use of *Ctrl + G.*

Secret #11. How to Find or Extract Unique Values[25]

1	Place your cursor over any cell in your range.
2	Select *Data* ⇨ *Advanced* (*Sort & Filter* Group).
3	Excel® automatically detects the *List Range*. Check the box to the left of *Unique records only*.
4	Tell Excel® what to do with the unique values: • If you select *Filter the list in place*, Excel® will hide the duplicate values in the same place • If you select *Copy to another location*, you need to indicate Excel® to which location. Do this by pointing to the destination cell in *Copy to*. Excel® will copy the unique values (all columns) headings and all!

Example

Your office party is coming up, and you want to bring a very intelligent date to show everyone how intelligent *you* are (yeah, well, a brilliant babe would obviously pick a brilliant dude like you, right? (You may have noticed I'm assuming you are a dude and you think you are brilliant. Well, since you're reading this book I guess you are brilliant.) So who should you

---

[25] You could also identify (and highlight) unique values (or even duplicate values) using conditional formatting, sure. Good thinking!

invite? You remember having read that women with big butts are proven to be smarter[26], and that men will always prefer a big J-Lo bottom than a pretty face[27]. So you decide to open up the list of dates you've had with women with those kinds of assets, extract the unique names and start calling[28].

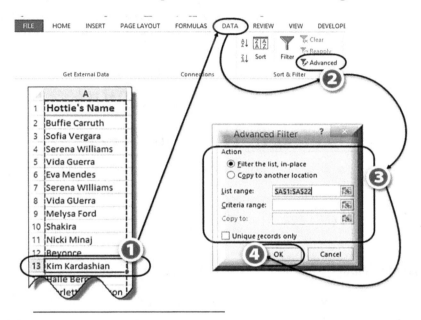

---

[26] Phalange (2013). Regina Phalange asserts that, "People with big butts are proven to be smarter and healthier!" and adds that, "A study at Oxford University showed that women with a phat butt were less likely to get diabetes, since they are more likely to produce hormones to metabolize sugar. It also showed that they are more likely to be intelligent."

[27] Abrahams (2014). Marlon Abrahams quotes Dr. Andrew Clark, a Specialist in Evolutionary Psychology at Bristol University, who explains that this has to do with genetic selection. Apparently when men look at a woman's big bottom, they (subconsciously) know that she is capable of bearing 'healthy and intelligent' children.

[28] This list includes real and imaginary dates.

1	Place your cursor on any cell in the list.
2	Select *Data* ⇨ *Advanced* ⇨ *Filter the list in place* ⇨ *Unique records only* ⇨ OK.

Shortcuts That Deal With Multiple Items at Once

Secret #12. Multiple Selection Shortcuts

How to Select Cells Faster with Your Keyboard

Shift: You may already know that you can press and hold the *Shift* key to select a range of cells, rows, or columns that are contiguous (which means they are next to one another.)

For instance, to select the range A1:C5 you could,

a. Click on A1 and holding the click button down slide your cursor down and to the right until it covers C5, so that the region A1:C5 is highlighted,

b. *Or*, you could click on A1, press and hold the *Shift* key, and click on C5. You have selected the "region" of adjacent cells.

Ctrl: You probably also already know that instead of *Shift*, pressing the *Ctrl* key allows you to select non-contiguous cells.

For instance, click on A1, press and hold the *Ctrl* key, and click on C5. You have selected *only* the two non-contiguous cells you clicked on: A1 and C5, and no other cell.

Keyboard shortcuts: Now here are a few more ways to select several cells fast.

Shift + Space	Select entire row.
Ctrl + Space	Select entire column.
Ctrl + Shift + Arrow	Extend selection to last cell with content in row (if you press the left or right arrow key) or column (if you press the up or down arrow.)
Shift + Home	Extend the selection to the beginning of the row.
Ctrl + Shift+*	Select entire active region[29].
Ctrl + a	If the active cell (the cell where the cursor is) is blank then *Ctrl + a* selects the entire sheet. If the active cell has data, then it selects the cell's region (like *Ctrl + Shift + **).

---

[29] A region is a group of cells that are separated from the rest of the universe by a blank row (or rows), a blank column (or columns), and/or the sheet's edge(s). Some people would call them "tables," but a table in Excel® is a different animal.

Example

The following illustrations show a third way of selecting a whole region (besides *Ctrl + a* and *Ctrl + Shift + **).

1	First, click on the top left corner of the region, then press *Ctrl + Shift + Right Arrow*. That selected the first row of data.
2	Then press *Ctrl + Shift + Down Arrow*. That selected every row all the way to the last one in your region. An easier way to select the region would have been to click on any of its cells and then press *Ctrl + A* (but then you wouldn't have been able to practice the *Ctrl + Shift + Arrow*.)

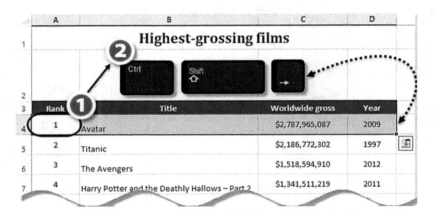

Mouse shortcuts: Here's still another way to select the active region (This is like adding the *Shift* key to Secret #43.)

1	Click on it to activate the upper left corner cell.
2	While holding down the *Shift* key, double click on the right border of the cell (this selects all the cells in this region to the right of the active one.)
3	Don't release the Shift key yet! Now double click on the bottom border of the cell (this selects every row below the active one in that region.)

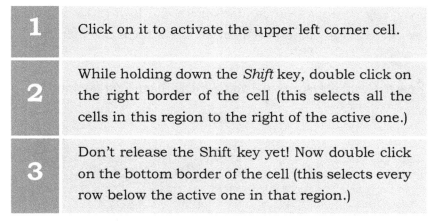

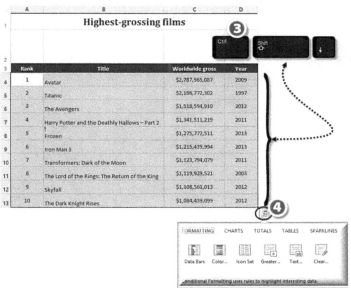

Secret #13. Multiple Autosum

With the *Quick Analysis Button* (new in Excel® 2013) calculating totals, percentages, etc. is easier than ever. Still, this Shortcut may help you total data a bit faster. Users who favor key combos over mouse clicks will love it. Let's look at the Shortcut and then we'll review the alternative method.

How to Calculate Horizontal and Vertical Sums Fast (Method #1)

2013 Quarterly Sales per City

City	Q1	Q2	Q3	Q4
Santa Claus, Indiana	$18,246	$19,220	$13,608	$32,890
Intercourse, Pennsylvania	$54,700	$62,349	$41,667	$50,918
Idiotville, Oregon	$17,923	$28,900	$38,912	$33,920
Knockemstiff, Ohio	$9,800	$10,230	$3,200	$12,678
Cut and Shoot, Texas	$28,727	$29,810	$319,023	$27,001

2013 Quarterly Sales per City

City	Q1	Q2	Q3	Q4	
Santa Claus, Indiana	$18,246	$19,220	$13,608	$32,890	$83,964
Intercourse, Pennsylvania	$54,700	$62,349	$41,667	$50,918	$209,634
Idiotville, Oregon	$17,923	$28,900	$38,912	$33,920	$119,655
Knockemstiff, Ohio	$9,800	$10,230	$3,200	$12,678	$35,908
Cut and Shoot, Texas	$28,727	$29,810	$319,023	$27,001	$404,561
	$129,396	$150,509	$416,410	$157,407	$853,722

1	Select the range you want to total, including an extra blank row for the vertical totals and an extra blank column for the horizontal totals.
2	Click on the *Autosum* button or press Alt =, as shown in the illustration above[30].

---

[30] These are real city names. To learn how they got those "unusual" names see Soniak, Matt and De Main, Bill (2014).

If you only want vertical (or only horizontal) totals (select only the cells where the totals will be – no need to select the numbers you want to add.

How to Calculate Horizontal and Vertical Sums Fast (Method #2)

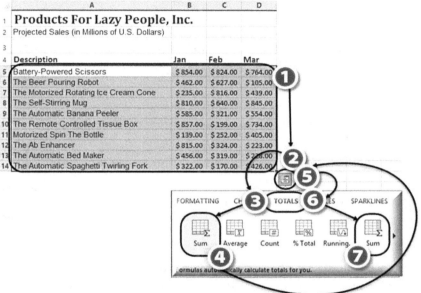

	Select the range you want to total. *The Quick Analysis Button* (QAB) pops up next to its bottom right corner.
1	

	Follow this sequence to calculate the vertical totals and then repeat it to calculate the horizontal totals (either order is fine): *Totals* tab ⇨ *Sum*
2	

Did you notice all the options this little guy (the QAB) offers you? Percentages, averages, counts, running totals, wow!

Secret #14. Viewing Multiple Sheets At Once[31]

These Shortcuts will let you view two or more sheets side by side. Once you've arranged them using any of the methods presented, switch between them using any of these methods:

- Press *Ctrl + Tab,* or

- Just click inside the window you want to go to, or

- *View* ⇨ *Switch Windows* ⇨ Click on the one you want

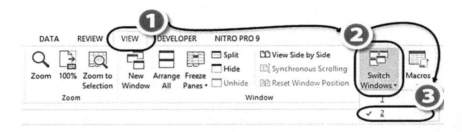

---

[31] In Excel 2013 each workbook opens in its own window and has its own Ribbon, formula bar, status bar, etc. In previous versions there was one "master" window and all books opened under its umbrella and shared one ribbon, one formula bar, one status bar, etc.

If you don't have or don't care about having two monitors feel free to leave this footnote now. You're done. Go, go. Now, working with two monitors was a pain in previous versions... for instance, the book on the left monitor would keep the ribbon, so the one on the right had no commands....Actually, some people solved this by opening two instances of Excel®, but the problem was that the copy-paste full functionality didn't work very well with two instances. So what people started doing instead of opening two instances was drinking a few tequilas every day on their way to work, so they could see two ribbons (the problem was that they also saw two bosses! Agghh!)

How to View Two Sheets from Different Books Side by Side

1	Make sure that (at least) the two workbooks that contain the two sheets you want to look at side-by-side are open.
2	By clicking on it, activate the first sheet you want to look at side-by-side with another.
3	Select *View* ⇨ *View Side by Side* (in the *Window* group). This command is not undoable.
4	If you only have two books open, go to step 5. If you have more than two, Excel® displays the *Compare Side by Side With* dialog box. Click on the name of the book that has the second sheet you want to look at and click OK.
5	If it's not active, activate the second sheet (in the second book) you want to look at by clicking on its name (in the list of sheet names at the bottom).
6	To scroll both sheets at the same time click on *View* ⇨ *Synchronous Scrolling* (*Windows* group).
7	To restore a window to full size click its *Maximize* icon (upper right corner).

How to View Two Sheets from the Same Book Side by Side

1	Let's first create a second window to look at the workbook from two windows: Select *View* ⇨ *New Window* (*Window* group).
2	Now select *View* ⇨ *View Side by Side* (in the *Window* group).
3	In each window select the worksheet you want to look at (it could be the same in both windows.)

How to View Multiple Sheets Simultaneously

1	Open all the workbooks that contain them, and in each book activate the sheet you want to look at.
2	Find the Excel icon on your *Windows Taskbar* (at the bottom of your screen[32]).

---

[32] If you haven't "pinned" Excel to the taskbar, why haven't you? Excuses, excuses, excuses! Okay, let's do it now. Fire up your Excel. When it's running, you'll see her icon on the taskbar. *Right-Click* on it and select *Pin this program to taskbar*. Works for Windows 7 or 8. In the future it'll be easier for you to boot Excel (just click on its icon on the taskbar), and it will also be easier to organize your open workbooks. Here's a trick for you, keyboard-lovers: let's say that Excel's is the 5th icon from the left on your taskbar, and that Word's is the 9th. You can switch from Word to Excel by pressing the *Windows* key (on your keyboard, the one with the Windows logo, usually to the left of the *Alt* key) and the number 5 at the same time.

3 Press *Shift* + *Right-click* on it. You get a menu (shown below) that allows you to cascade them, show them stacked, show them side by side, restore them, minimize them, or close them all.

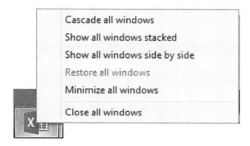

You can also use *View* ⇨ *Arrange All* (*Window* group) ⇨ *Tiled, Horizontal, Vertical or Cascade*. Notice the check box to the left of *Windows of Active workbook* that allows you to avoid including windows from other workbooks.

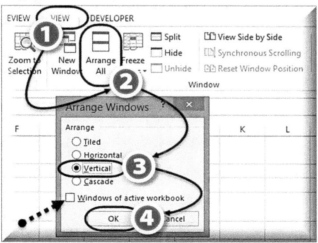

Then you can switch back to Word by pressing the Windows key and the number 9. Fast, huh?

Wanna try something cool? Select one or several cells in a sheet and *move them* into another sheet using your mouse (click and drag)! Much easier than cutting them (*Ctrl + C*), going into the second sheet, and pasting them (*Enter*), huh?

Secret #15. Opening Multiple Files at Once[33]

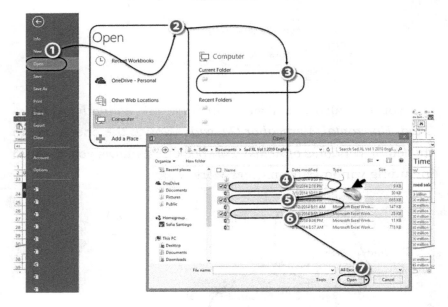

| **1** | Select *File ⇨ Open*. |

---

33 In previous versions of Excel you could save (and later open) several workbooks at the same time (as well as their physical arrangement) by saving your "workspace." That feature is no longer available in 2013.

| 2 | Navigate your folder's structure until you find the first file you want to open. Click on its name once. |

| 3 | Holding down the *Ctrl* key, click on the name of the next file you want to open. |

| 4 | Repeat Step 3 for every file you want to open. |

| 5 | Click *OK*. |

Secret #16. Multiple Copy-Pastes

You may have heard of "The Clipboard." Here's what most people know:

| 1 | You select an object(s) you want to duplicate. |

| 2 | You press *Ctrl + C* or click on *Home* ⇨ *Copy*. |

| 3 | You select a place (or several places) where you want to get the duplicate(s). |

| 4 | You hit *Enter*, press *Ctrl + V*, or click on *Home* ⇨ *Paste*. |

And that's how *you* duplicate objects, such as cells, charts, shapes, etc[34]. Most people think that, once you've copied something into the clipboard, you need to "pull it out" (by pasting it somewhere) before you can copy something else. That would mean that the clipboard can only hold one "thing" at a time. Not true.

You can perform several *Copy* operations (up to 24) and the objects that you send to the clipboard will be saved, all of them, so that later you can retrieve as many duplicates as you want of any of them, in any order, and into any Microsoft Office® application document.

Visualize the clipboard as a *jar* where you can put "stuff" and it lays on top of what you've put there previously. Actually, to put things into it, to pull things out of it, or to see its contents you need to open the jar (duh). Don't duh me, because this jar is *transparent*[35].

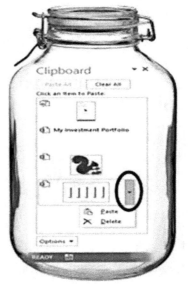

---

[34] Instead of clicking *Ctrl + C*, some people right click and select *Copy*. That's fine too.

[35] Actually, the technical story is this: there are two clipboards, the Windows one, which is the one that most people know and use, and the Office one, which is the jar you've got to open to use... and they pass things from one another, and they have rules, blah, blah. That story is not as exciting, so never mind.

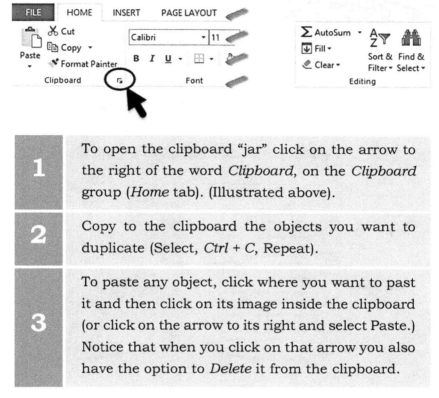

1	To open the clipboard "jar" click on the arrow to the right of the word *Clipboard*, on the *Clipboard* group (*Home* tab). (Illustrated above).
2	Copy to the clipboard the objects you want to duplicate (Select, *Ctrl + C*, Repeat).
3	To paste any object, click where you want to past it and then click on its image inside the clipboard (or click on the arrow to its right and select Paste.) Notice that when you click on that arrow you also have the option to *Delete* it from the clipboard.

Isn't it pretty cool?

It gets better: not only can you "pull" objects out of the jar in any order you want, but the clipboard is shared by different applications! So next time you want to prepare a PowerPoint® presentation with data from Excel® and Word® for instance, open all of them, go into Excel® and place "stuff" into the clipboard, then go to Word® and do the same, and finally go to your PowerPoint® and start "pulling" duplicates of the stuff you placed there as needed.

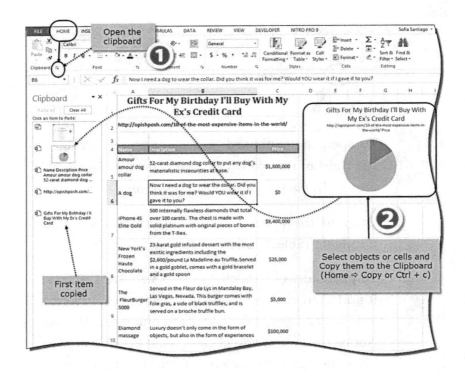

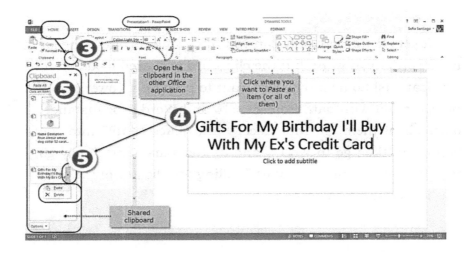

Careful with Formulas

When you copy a formula "the old way" (with your *Ctrl + C*
⇨ *Enter* or *Ctrl + V)* you're actually getting a duplicate of the
formula itself. In contrast, with this new method the paste is
like a *Paste* ⇨ *Value,* so you get the *result,* not the formula.

Secret #17. Multiple Undos

Most people have used the *Undo* at least once[36], either by
clicking on its icon on their *Quick Access Toolbar,* or by
pressing *Ctrl + Z.* But what if you royally screwed up? Not
many people know about the *multiple Undos.*

Next time you want to *Undo several* actions, instead of
going *Undo-Undo-Undo-Undo,* which quite frankly looks as silly
as it sounds, do this:

> **1** Click on the drop down arrow to the right of the
> *Undo* icon. Excel® displays a list of up to 100 with
> the most-recent undoable-tasks you've carried
> out, with the most-recent at the top.

---

[36] I'd be willing to bet that it's in the Guinness Book of World Records
as the most used spreadsheet command in the history of the world.
Come on, be honest: have you ever wanted your sweetie to have a
button equivalent to Excel®'s Undo? You know, a button in an easily
accessible place (perhaps on their nose) where you could just click
with your finger (Click!) and it would magically delete the last action
you did, as if it had never happened?

2 As you move your mouse pointer over the list, Excel® highlights the task you're hovering over and the ones you've performed afterwards. Highlight the oldest one you want to undo and *Click.*

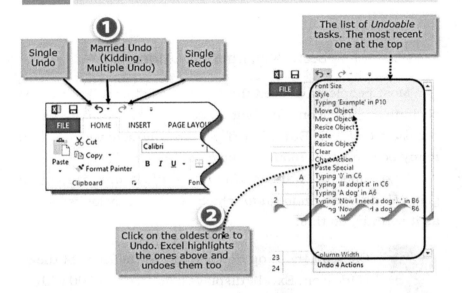

The list of *Undoable* tasks. The most recent one at the top

Single Undo

Married Undo (Kidding. Multiple Undo)

Single Redo

Click on the oldest one to Undo. Excel highlights the ones above and undoes them too

I know what you're thinking. The answer is no, sorry — there's no such thing as a *selective Undo*. It was a good question, though. Oh, and a few other warnings:

- Excel® doesn't warn you when an action you're about to undertake is undoable (but then again, what chick would?)

- *Macros*[37] are not undoable.

---

[37] To learn about macros and how to create them please read Volume 2.

- You know when you open an old file, modify it, and intend to save the new version with a new name, but you forget to pick *Save as* and just click *Save*.... And then, less than one tenth of a second after you clicked, you go "SH.... aving cream!" because you realize what you did? Yeah, well. That kind of mess in not undoable either.

Shortcuts to Enter Data Way Faster

Secret #18. How to Save a Lot of Clicks When Entering Data

What key do *you* press after typing data so it'll enter into the cell? Are you a "taber," an "arrower," or an "enterer"? Or an "all-of-the-above-er"? Perhaps you have multiple personality disorder and switch all the time. In that case, you may be saying, "Well, I use *tab* when filling data by row, and when I reach the end of the row I hit *Enter* so Excel® will automatically bring me to the leftmost cell in the next row," as the next illustration shows. Wow! I'm impressed! You're already saving a lot of clicks!

Tab-Tab-Tab-Tabbing

1	*Before* entering values, select the area where you want to input the data into (the cells don't need to be contiguous —they can be all over, just use *Shift* and/or *Ctrl* to select them[38].)
2	Type the first value. DON'T hit *Enter*. Press *Tab*. This enters the data and moves your cursor to the next cell within the input area you pre-selected.
3	Keep moving to the next cell using the *Tab* key.

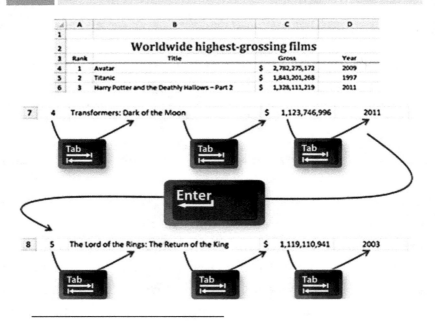

---

[38] Optionally, type a name for this area in the *Name Box*. This way you'll be able to select it in the future just by selecting its name in the *Name box's drop down list*. Don't remember where it is? It's illustrated on Secret #50.

Secret #19. How to Enter Data into Multiple Cells at Once

1 Easy. *Select* the cells you want to enter the same data into (it can be a value or a formula.)

2 *Type* the value. Excel® shows it as if you were entering it into the active cell only—Pretend she's your spouse and just ignore her.

3 Use *Ctrl + Enter* instead of *Enter*, *Tab*, or an *arrow* key to finish entering it.

Other Great Uses for *Ctrl + Enter*

- You can use these same three steps when you're *modifying* (or editing) data instead of just entering it for the first time.

- You can also use the *Ctrl + Enter* combo to keep the same cell as the *active cell* after entering data into it. In other words, if you use the *Enter* key alone to finish inputting data into a cell, *by default* Excel® enters the data and moves the cursor down one cell, so the cell below the one you entered data into becomes the new active cell. Not if you replace the *Enter* with *Ctrl + Enter*. Very useful when you plan to immediately process that cell further, such as by formatting it, autofilling it, etc.

Example

Imagine you're in charge of an Employee Absence sheet (like the one below). The first column is a list of your employee's names. The next 12 columns, labeled Jan, Feb, Mar, and so on correspond to…. Take a guess. Right! The 12 months of the year, good job!

In the cell that corresponds to the row labeled "Anita Beer" and to the column "May," for instance, you've typed a number that shows how many days Anita Beer missed work in May. At this point you've recorded everyone's absences, and now you want to fill the blank spaces with a dash (you prefer the "Sheet Chic" style.) We'll use *Ctrl + G Special* to select all of the blank cells in the range, and then we'll use *Ctrl + Enter* to enter a dash into all of them simultaneously.

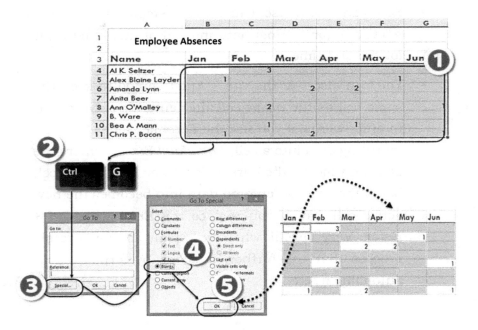

1	Select the range that includes the blank cells.
2	Press *Ctrl + G.*
3	Click on the *Special* button (bottom left corner).
4	Click on *Blanks.*
5	Type a dash (-).
6	Press *Ctrl + Enter.*

Secret #20. How to Create a Drop-Down List

| 1 | Enter the list of values you want to display in a drop down into any sheet[39]. |
| 2 | Select the range of cells where you'll want to display the drop down list (it may be in the same sheet than the list but that's not necessary.) |

---

[39] For instance a list of state abbreviations, such as AL, CA, PO, NE, err.... PO? Let's delete that one – I'm not sure that's a state... Type them in the order you want them to be displayed in the drop-down.

3	Click on *Data* ⇨ *Data Validation* (in the *Data Tools* Group) ⇨ *Settings* Tab (Selected by default).
4	Indicate Excel to *Allow* values from a list by selecting that word (*List*) under *Allow*.
5	Click below the word *Source*. Select the range with the list of values, wherever it is (navigate to a different sheet if necessary –just click on the sheet's name at the bottom of your screen, just above the status bar, and then select the range.)
6	Click *OK*.

Here's a best practice for those of you who are visionaries. If you anticipate that your list will grow, select the whole column that contains it as the *Source*, rather than just the range that currently holds values. To select a whole column click on its header (letter). That way, if you later add more elements down below the current ones you won't need to modify the data validation rule you're establishing. Smart, huh? I bet this is what guys like Jules Verne, Leonardo Da Vinci and Steve Jobs did whenever they created drop-downs.

Example

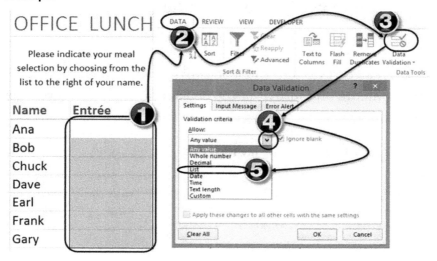

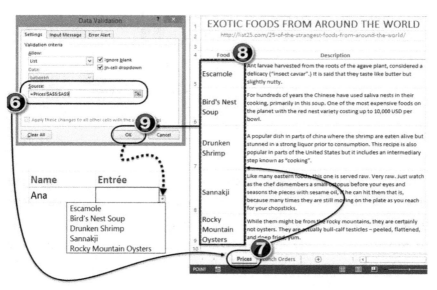

Secret #21. How to Repeat the Previous Row's Entry

Press *Ctrl + D* and you'll be copying into the selected cell(s) the contents and format of the cell(s) immediately above it (or them).

	A	B	C	D	E
1	**People I Won't Invite to My Next Party**				
2					
3	Who	Street	City/County	State	Country
4	Any resident of	Divorce Court	Heather Highlands	Pennsylvania	USA
5	Any resident of	Psycho Path	Traverse City	Michigan	USA
6	Any resident of	This Ain't It Road	Alexander City	Alabama	USA
7	Any resident of	No Name Street	Turnersville	New Jersey	USA
8	Any resident of	Wong Way	Riverside	California	USA
9	Any resident of	Zzyzx Road	San Bernardino	California	USA
10	Any resident of	Cannibal Road	Loleta		

❶

❷ **Ctrl** **D**

	A	B	C	D	E
9	Any resident of	Zzyzx Road	San Bernardino	California	USA
10	Any resident of	Cannibal Road	Loleta	California	USA

This shortcut is very useful when you're entering rows and rows of data where some information is repetitive. The illustration shows you how this works as well when you want to repeat the values in more than one cell[40]. Now it's time for an IQ test. Complete the following sentence: I use *Ctrl D* to fill *Down*, so to fill *Right* I'll use *Ctrl* ___[41]?

---

[40] Murano (2009) and Squiddo (2014). These are real street names.

[41] If you answered R, you RRRRRRock!!

Secret #22. How to Create a Spin Button

Whether a spin button will make your data entry faster or not is debatable, but it will definitely bring your form closer to a Rodeo Drive-Chic look than to a Walmart-Chic look In this example we'll draw spin buttons to control cells F8 and G8[42].

Look at the previous illustration. In this example, cell F8 shows the credit card expiration month and G8 shows the card's expiration year. Instead of typing those two numbers, the users of this form will click on the arrows to increase or decrease the numbers shown in the corresponding cells.

---

[42] The spin button will *not* be *inside* the cells. Remember a cell can only contain a number, a text, a date (which is actually saved as a number), or a formula (sparklines, the little charts that fit inside a cell are actually saved as formulas, I think...), but not a "form control." Spin buttons are form controls, so as I said, don't think of them as being inside cells. Instead, picture them floating on top of cells, kind of like on a transparent layer placed on top of the cells, the same way your screen protector is placed on top of your smartphone.

1	First, make sure that the *Developers* tab is visible on *The Ribbon* (steps on page 40).
2	Do *Developer* ⇨ *Insert* ⇨ *Spin button* (top row icon, third one from right to left). Draw a small spin button covering approximately the third right side of the cell where the number it will control will be displayed. The spin button is selected, so you can move it or resize it like any other object. If it gets de-selected just *Ctrl + Click* on it to select it again[43].
3	Right click on the spin button. If you get a short menu with three options (*Move here, Copy here, or Cancel*), right click again and again on the button until you get the long menu that includes the command *Format Control* (as illustrated).
4	Select the last option: *Format Control*. Fill the data in the *Control* tab as shown on the next page.

---

[43] You'll know you've effectively selected the button and not the cell behind it if you see a frame with white little circles (the selection handles) around it (as illustrated on the next page). If you don't see them try right clicking again on a slightly different location, closer to the center of the button. Try again until you get the handles.

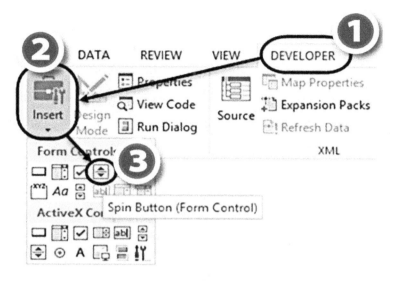

Current value: The number that the cell will initially display. We'll type 6 (middle point between 1 and 12 to be fair to users who need a month in the second semester). You should pick the most common value to be the "default." **Minimum**: 1 (January). **Maximum**: 12 (December). **Increments**: 1 unit. **Cell Link:** In this case F8. It's the reference to the cell that's behind the spin button (which is the one that it controls.)

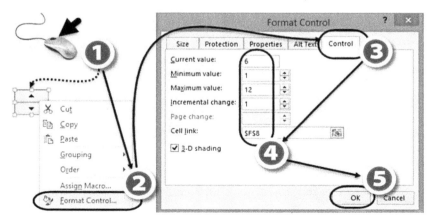

5	Left align the contents of the *cell link* (F8) so the spin button won't cover the number: select F8, *Home* ⇨ *Align* left icon in the *Alignment* group.
6	For your form to look nicer, you can hide the gridlines: *View* ⇨ uncheck *Gridlines* (in the *Show* group[44]).

---

[44] You can also hide all the empty columns to the right of your form, and all the empty rows below it. Here's how: imagine your form is in A1:D12. We'll leave row 13 and column E blank, like a frame.

(1) Click on the letter F to select column F (makes sense!)

(2) Press *Ctrl + Shift + Right arrow* to select all the columns to the right all the way to the end of the world.

(3) *Right click* ⇨ *Hide*.

(4) Now let's hide the blank rows. Click on the number 14 to the left of row 14

(5) Press *Ctrl + Shift + Down arrow*.

(6) *Right click* ⇨ *Hide*. Voila.

If you ever decide to *Unhide* those columns and/or rows, here's a secret you'll need to know: select every cell by clicking on the square to the left of column A and above row 1 (right underneath the *Name Box*), and then

(1) Without clicking, place the mouse pointer over any row number and *Right click* ⇨ *Unhide* to unhide all the hidden rows.

(2) Without clicking, place the mouse pointer over any column letter and *Right click* ⇨ *Unhide* to unhide all the hidden columns.

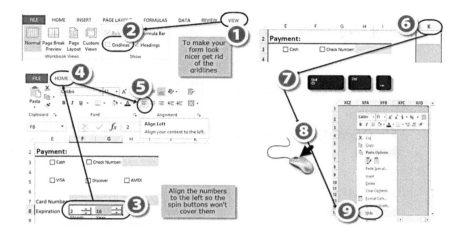

To draw the other controls shown on this form, which are check marks, just go to *Developer* ⇨ *Insert* ⇨ *Check Box* ⇨ click where you want the control. Then right click on it and *Edit Text* to edit its caption.

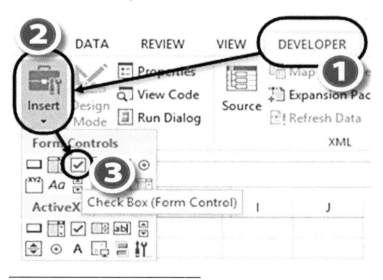

OMG, you don't know this, but I know you would have gone crazy trying to figure out what to select in order to unhide them if I hadn't told you this! HA!

Secret #23. Enter Zip Codes, Phones, or SSNs Fast[45]

1	Select the cells where you'll enter these numbers.
2	Open the *Format* Dialog Box (See Secret #45.) On the *Number* tab select *Special.*
4	Click on the type of format you want out of the four options menu: *Zip, Zip + 4, Phone Number,* or *Social Security Number.*
5	Click *OK.*
6	Type the numbers without dashes or leading zeroes.

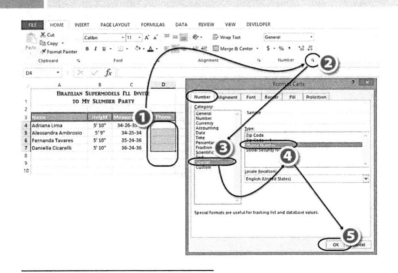

---

45 Excel® has built-in formats for these types of data. See how smart she is? She anticipates your needs!

You can apply the special format *before* or after entering data. If you do it before though, the numbers you enter will be immediately displayed with the right format.

Secret #24. How to Enter Data Through a Cool-Beans Form

The *Form* command displays a nice looking *form*[46] to help you enter or delete records from your "database" one at a time. It also allows you to browse through your records, and even to find those that meet specific criteria you establish.

Let's try it with this database, where each record (row) has information about one brand of beer.

This command is not in *The Ribbon*, so the first six steps of the process will allow us to find it and add it to our *Quick Access Toolbar*[47], so we can then use it.

---

[46] Really??

[47] There's a *Customizing the QAT 101* lesson on Shortcut #6.

	A	B	C	D	E
1	**The worst beer in the world**				
2	As rated by the thousands of beer enthusiasts at RateBeer.com				
3					
4	Rank	Beer	Score	Count	Style
5	1	Natural Light	1.04	1179	Amber Ale
6	2	Natural Ice	1.06	837	Strong Ale
7	3	Milwaukee's Best Premium	1.08	843	Brown Ale
8	4	Michelob Ultra	1.09	1222	Dark Ale
9	5	Sleeman Clear	1.09	136	Imperial Strong
10	6	Olde English 800 3.2	1.11	82	Malt Liquor
11	7	Budweiser Select 55	1.14	199	Imperial Stout
12	8	Busch Ice	1.15	163	Pale Lager
13	9	Bud Light Chelada	1.16	302	Spice/Herb/Vegetable
14	10	Milwaukee's Best Light	1.17	501	Pale Lager

1	Click on the drop down arrow on the right side of the *Quick Access Toolbar.*
2	Select *More Commands.* The *Customize the QAT* dialog box opens up. On the left side you can see all the commands you can add to the QAT, organized by categories. On the right side you see another box with the commands that are already in the *QAT.*
3	Select the category *All commands*[48] by clicking on the drop down arrow to the right of *Choose commands from* (top left).

---

[48] You could also select *Commands not in the Ribbon.*

4 In the alphabetical list of commands, find *Form* and click on it.

5 Click on the *Add* button that's in the center. Now you see it on the right side list.

6 Click OK. The *Form* command is now sitting on your QAT, waiting for you to use it.

7 Click on any cell in your database.

8 Click on the *Form* command icon on the QAT. A form opens up. Its caption (top left corner) is the name of the active sheet, and it has several buttons to perform the operations described in the following summary.

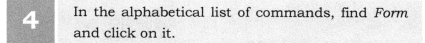

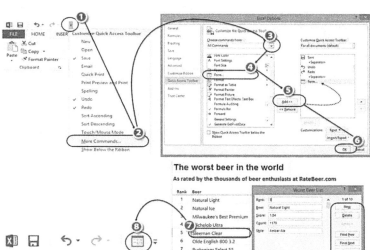

The worst beer in the world

As rated by the thousands of beer enthusiasts at RateBeer.com

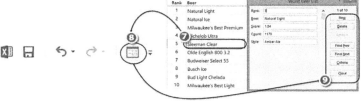

To add a new record after the last one	Click *New,* Enter the data, Click *New* again.
To delete a record	Display it. Click on the *Delete* button (not undoable).
To undo changes made to a record	Click on the Restore button. This only works if the changes were made through this form, and if you haven't moved out of the record yet.
To navigate one record at a time	Click on the *Find Prev* or *Find Next* buttons.
To find records with specific values in any column	Click on the *Criteria* button. Type the values you're looking for in the field that's named after the column where they should be at. Press *Enter* and Excel® shows you the next one (from where she was at) that meets that criteria. Navigate through the rest using *Find Prev* and *Find Next.* End the "filter" with *Criteria* ⇨ *Clear* ⇨ *Form.* When filling the criteria values you can use the two wildcards star and quotation mark. Use * to replace several characters and ?

	to replace one character. For instance:
	Light would display all beers that end in Light.
	???? Ale would pick Dark Ale, but not Amber Ale, or Strong Ale (four quotation marks require only four characters, as in Dark, but not in Amber or Strong, which are five and six-letter words respectively.
What the Close button does to the cool-beans form	I'm not writing anymore. This has been too much work already, so you'll have to figure this one out on your own.

The Black Little Square

Basic Concepts

Have you noticed how the shape of Excel®'s mouse pointer changes depending on which part of a cell you hover it over?

- When you hover it over the cell's frame, it turns into a four-headed black arrow

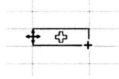

- When you hover it over the bottom right corner of the cell, it turns into a black cross (like a plus symbol, you got it).

- Everywhere else it looks like a fat white cross.

The Thingy

That bottom right corner of the active cell, the black square that turns your cursor into a 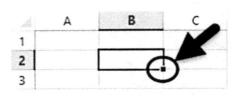 black cross, has two technical names: (1) The autofill handle, and (2) The Thingy. If you click on it and drag it, it copies or fills the contents of the active cell into the adjacent ones in the direction in which you pull it.

Example

- Place your cursor on any cell.
- Type the three letters j a n (no spaces in between please, and don't hit *Enter*[49].
- Hover your cursor over The Thingy. When the cursor turns into a black cross, click and hold.
- Holding down the mouse click button move your cursor to the right slowly, so you can see that as you extend your selection to include the next cell the word feb appears in a tip box below your selection.

---

[49] Oh, how perceptive of you to realize you're typing the first three letters of January!

- Keep holding the click button, and move again in the same direction to extend the selection a few more cells. Notice how Excel® is automatically filling the months for you (Aha!)

- Once you've filled as many elements as you want, release the click (just let go. Ahh...)

Details on the Autofill Feature

A few things to notice from the previous example:

- We didn't need to start in January. We could have started on any month (Excel® would have taken it from there.)

- Excel® autofills using the same capitalization as the "seed" (if our seed had been JAN, she'd have gone on with FEB, MAR; if we had given her Jan, she'd have filled Feb, Mar...)

- If you Autofill more cells than the number of elements in the list, Excel® starts recreating the list from the seed and on (here, if you had Autofilled more than 11 cells she would've restarted with Jan.)

- The two pre-defined lists Excel® knows by heart are months and days (full name or first three letters), but we can teach her any list we want her to remember.

Thingying Stuff[50]

In any case, every cell has a *thingy* you can pull, which means you can *autofill* any cell's content. However, the results you'll get will depend on:

a. The type of data you're autofilling, and

b. On whether or not you're using one of the shortcuts described in the next section.

In the worksheet shown below I entered data only into the first row, and then I used the autofill feature to fill down the rest of the data in rows 2 to 8. Each column has a different type of "seed." Notice what Excel® autofills in each case.

	A	B	C	D	E	F	G	H	I
1	1	My name	Team 1	1/1/2014	=A1*2	March	Jul	Monday	Sat
2	1	My name	Team 2	1/2/2014	=A2*2	April	Aug	Tuesday	Sun
3	1	My name	Team 3	1/3/2014	=A3*2	May	Sep	Wednesday	Mon
4	1	My name	Team 4	1/4/2014	=A4*2	June	Oct	Thursday	Tue
5	1	My name	Team 5	1/5/2014	=A5*2	July	Nov	Friday	Wed
6	1	My name	Team 6	1/6/2014	=A6*2	August	Dec	Saturday	Thu
7	1	My name	Team 7	1/7/2014	=A7*2	September	Jan	Sunday	Fri
8	1	My name	Team 8	1/8/2014	=A8*2	October	Feb	Monday	Sat

---

50 I'll use the action verb "*Thingying*" in reference to autofilling because its shorter than "clicking on the autofill handle and dragging it."

By default (no shortcut) this is what Excel® does:

If the seed is	Autofill gives you[51]	Examples
A number or a text	A copy or copies of the seed	Columns A and B
A text that ends in a number	A series where each element has the me text, but the number is incremented ' one unit each time	Column C
A date	A series in increments of one day	Column D
A formula	A copy of the formula, adjusting the relative references[52]	Column E
A list	The next element(s) in that list. Excel® already knows the list of months and the list of days, but you can teach her any other list you want her to autofill, and she will!	Columns F, G, H and I above

Secret #25. Double Click the Thingy

After you've entered the contents in the seed-cell, instead of clicking and dragging (or pulling) *The Thingy,* you can just double click on it and Excel® automatically autofills down.

Double clicking The Thingy only works:

- To fill down (not in any other direction).

---

51 If you want something else, read Secrets #28 and #30.

52 For details on relative versus absolute references read Volume 2.

- When there is a column *with data* immediately to the left or to the right of the column where you're autofilling. Excel® needs this column's data as a reference to know how many rows down you want her to *autofill* before stopping.

Do you see how smart she is? She knows how far down to go. Actually, this shortcut also confirms that, in fact, Excel® is female: she will not honor a request that is unreasonable.

Here's what I mean. For instance, if you double clicked a thingy in the middle of nowhere[53] expecting Excel® to read your mind and know how far down you want her to go, she wouldn't do it.

See?

Some of you readers are used to having to pull *The Thingy* down to copy data (especially to copy formulas) to hundreds and even thousands of rows, am I right? What do you mean you don't know? Ah, never mind. This shortcut is *HUGE* for users who manipulate *HUGE* spreadsheets.

Been there, done that. And if you're as impatient as I am, you grab *The Thingy*, slide your mouse down to fill down, and.... Oops! You've gone too far down—you're probably close to cell one million! So without releasing the click button, you move your cursor up, and ... Oops! When you notice, you've gone too far up —you're close to the first rows of data. So you correct course once more and go down... And up... And down.... And up... And when you notice, you've spent half your morning playing yoyo with *The Thingy*! No more.

---

[53] I'm referring to the Autofill handle of a cell that is surrounded by blank cells.

Secret #26. Create Sequences or Patterns

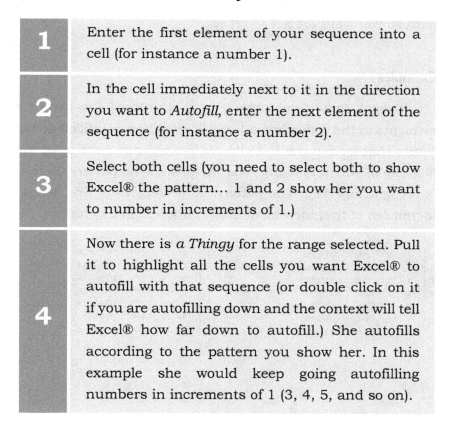

1	Enter the first element of your sequence into a cell (for instance a number 1).
2	In the cell immediately next to it in the direction you want to *Autofill,* enter the next element of the sequence (for instance a number 2).
3	Select both cells (you need to select both to show Excel® the pattern... 1 and 2 show her you want to number in increments of 1.)
4	Now there is *a Thingy* for the range selected. Pull it to highlight all the cells you want Excel® to autofill with that sequence (or double click on it if you are autofilling down and the context will tell Excel® how far down to autofill.) She autofills according to the pattern you show her. In this example she would keep going autofilling numbers in increments of 1 (3, 4, 5, and so on).

If in steps 1 and 2 above we had entered the numbers 2 and 4 respectively, Excel® would have kept autofilling the sequence in increments of 2 (6, 8, 10.... Do *you* know how to do this? Good.)

You can teach Excel® patterns by selecting more than two cells. Just highlight as many as necessary so she'll find the pattern you want for her to repeat[54].

Examples

In each one of columns A to D, I entered the two first elements in the series (rows 1 and 2) and then autofilled down. Notice that for column E, I selected not two but three cells, the last one of which is blank. Wanna guess what pattern Excel® is recognizing? Yep. The pattern is "increment of five, blank, increment of five, increment of five, blank," and so on.

	A	B	C	D	E
1	1	1	25%	1/1/2014	5
2	2	3	50%	1/8/2014	10
3	3	5	75%	1/15/2014	
4	4	7	100%	1/22/2014	
5	5	9	125%	1/29/2014	
6	6	11	150%	2/5/2014	
7	7	13	175%	2/12/2014	

	A	B	C	D	E
1	1	1	25%	1/1/2014	5
2	2	3	50%	1/8/2014	10
3	3	5	75%	1/15/2014	
4	4	7	100%	1/22/2014	15
5	5	9	125%	1/29/2014	20
6	6	11	150%	2/5/2014	
7	7	13	175%	2/12/2014	25
8					

---

[54] Example: for Excel to fill a list of dates that would include only Mondays, Wednesdays, and Fridays, you'd need to show her the first six elements: Monday, Wednesday, Friday, Monday, Wednesday, and Friday. That's because if you only gave her three elements, the next one she would fill (logically) would be Sunday (and then Tuesday and Thursday). Get it? She'd understand that what you wanted for her to do would be to list a day, skip a day, list a day, skip a day, and so on. Test your patterns before concluding she' doesn't understand you!

Wanna guess another pattern? Okay. Look at this "before" sheet and tell me what the "after" will look like:

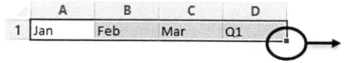

Yes, I typed Jan, autofilled Feb and Mar and then typed Q1. Then I selected A1:D1.

Did you guess right? Let's see.

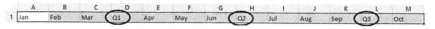

Excel® filled Apr, May, Jun, Q2, Jul, Aug, Sep, Q3, Oct, and would have gone on with Nov, Dec, and Q4. Wow!

Isn't that an interesting trick? It seems like Excel® is autofilling two interspersed series (months and quarters). Seriously, *anything* capable of this level of pattern recognition *has* to be female.

Oh, before I wrap up this Shortcut, a question I get quite frequently is this: Will this feature work to autofill patterns of dates? And my answer is, "Now that you know Excel® is female, do you think she will be able to do it?" And inevitably people answer their own question with an emphatic "Of course!" (If you know how to ask her *nicely*.)

Let's say you want to fill a list of Mondays, with the first one being 6/23/2014. Type this as a seed in one cell, type the next Monday in the next cell (6/30/2014), select both cells, and pull The Thingy[55]!

---

[55] Some of you are thinking, "Oh, I would have done it by entering a formula in the second cell (=first cell + 7) and then pulling that formula down. Sure, that would have worked too. It would actually

Secret #27. List Only Weekdays

Immediately after you autofilled a range, a small icon pops up next to the bottom right corner of the autofilled area (it's shown in the image below, next to the number for step 3.) It's called *Autofill Options*. Click on it and you get a menu that allows you to override the way Excel® autofills by default.

Example

Let's say you're creating a *Designated Texter*[56] *Schedule* for the four palindromicly-named-vehicularly-challenged-coworkers that ride with you every day. Their names are the

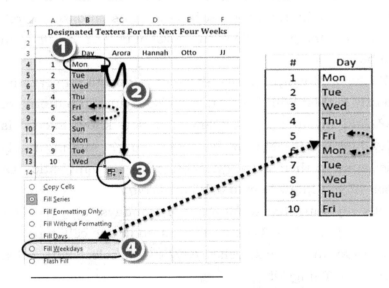

be a better way to do it if you think your "seed" (first date) will change, so good job!

---

[56] A passenger who reads and replies to any and all text messages received on the driver's phone, thus allowing the driver to focus on the road. Definition from urbandictionary.com.

column headings: Arora, Hannah, Otto, and JJ (Bob changed his name to "Bob, The Bombshell" and decided to change careers after he watched the movie Magic Mike, so no Bob.)

- Enter the title and headings as illustrated[57].

- Enter the numbers 1 and 2 into cells A4 and A5.

- Pull The Thingy watching the little numbering tip that Excel® displays so you'll know when you reach 20. Stop Thingying.

- Enter Mon into cell B4.

- Double click on B4's thingy. Excel filled 20 days, including Sats and Suns. Don't get distracted here! Do the next step before anything else!

- Click on the *Autofill options* icon .

- Click on the option button for *Fill Weekdays*.

The Autofill Options icon

- The autofill options icon is visible immediately after you Autofill. If you get distracted and go enter some other data, or widen the column because the Autofill threw a bunch of pounds at you (######), the icon won't be waiting for you (going to get a drink is okay.) Have you heard of "Use it or..."?

- If you were autofilling numbers, or a sequence of numbers, the options would be *Copy* cells, *Fill Series*, *Fill Formatting Only*, and *Fill Without Formatting*. For dates, the Autofill option has more —err— options (*Fill Months* or *Fill Years*).

---

[57] Unless your coworkers have different names.

- Notice the first option: *Copy* cells. So next time you want Excel to *copy* the same date instead of filling the series, you know what to do (No, if you said, "Call IT..?" think again.)

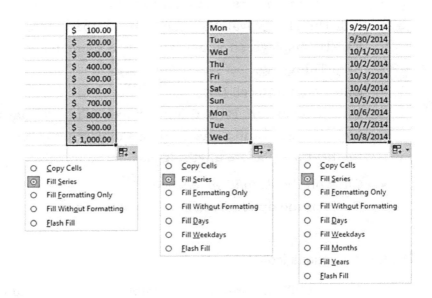

Secret #28. Right Click-Thingying

Be honest. If I had titled this Shortcut *Create Linear or Growth Trends*, or *Deciphering Ambiguous Patterns*, that would have scared you away, right? Believe me, I know.

Notice what happens when, *instead* of *clicking* on *The Thingy* and dragging it down, I do it with the *right-mouse-click* (instead of with the left). That's right. When you right-click-and-then-drag *The Thingy*:

- The *Autofill options* is automatically open when you finish autofilling, and

- The menu has *more* options. Some are grayed out, depending on whether you're autofilling dates or numbers.

- Notice the results (shown and charted on the right side of each option) of having Excel® follow a *linear trend* versus a *growth trend* when autofilling the series.

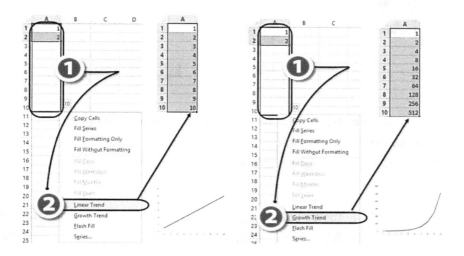

How many other women do you know that, when asked, "Hey honey, please gimme the next number in this sequence: 1... 2...?" would reply with, "If you want the linear trend that's 3, but if you want the growth trend, then 4. Would you like more dessert dear?" BAM!

Secret #29. Shift-Thingying

Shift-Thingying is a shortcut for inserting one or more blank cells below the one(s) selected.

Here's an example. Your birthday is approaching, so you decide to create a wish list to give your boss and coworkers.

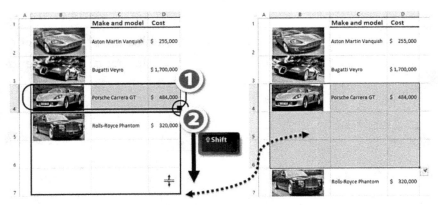

You're done entering the first four items, when you decide you want to add a couple more between the second and the third. This is how you'd do it by *Shift-Thingying.*

1	Select the cells below which you want to add the new blank cells (B3:D3).
2	Press and hold the *Shift* key. When you hover your mouse over the selection's *Thingy* it looks like a vertical double headed arrow with a double line crossing it in the middle.
3	Keep the *Shift* pressed. Click on The Thingy and drag it down two rows. Then let go[58].

---

[58] As you know, sometimes Excel® offers you more than one way to get the same result, so you get to choose. In this case, you could have accomplished the same by using any of these other methods:

Secret #30. Ctrl-Thingying

Ctrl-Thingying allows you to have Excel® do *the opposite* of what she would normally do when autofilling. When you press and hold the *Ctrl* key, and then Autofill cells, you're *overriding* Excel®'s defaults.

Look:

If the seed is	Autofill gives you this	Ctrl + Autofill gives you this instead
A number	A copy or copies of the seed	Excel® fills a series in increments of one
A text that ends in a number	A series. Same text. The number is incremented by one unit each time	A copy or copies of the seed
A date	A series of dates in increments of one day	A copy or copies of the seed
A list	The next element(s) in that list.	A copy or copies of the seed

Ctrl-Thingying a text or a formula is the same as just *pulling The Thingy without Ctrl* (Ouch!!)

(a) Instead of steps 2-4 above, you could have used the *Insert* command: *Home* ⇨ *Insert* ⇨ *Insert Cells* ⇨ *Shift cells down* or *Entire Row* (depending on whether there's other data in row 3).

(b) Instead of clicking on the *Insert* command (*Home* tab), you could have *right clicked* and selected it from the menu that pops up.

Don't *double-click* The Thingy though—it doesn't work. You have to pull it manually.

Secret #31. Create a List and Sort by It

Let's create the list first

One day you realized that you were wasting tons of time typing the names of your team members into different sheets (nominations for bonuses, birthdays, picnic planning, project schedules, new year's presents, your will, etc.) so you created a sheet where you typed the names, and now instead of typing the list every time you want it, you just open that file and copy-paste it. Well, there's a better way. Why not have Excel® memorize your list[59], just like she has memorized the list of months, so that you can use the *Autofill* feature to enter it anytime you need it, instead of going through all the work of opening another file and copy-pasting?

Yeah, why not?

Remembering that Excel® is female, and therefore smart enough to learn anything you know how to teach her *nicely*, you went ahead and typed the names of your coworkers in a new sheet, and you sorted them alphabetically.

But then you thought, wouldn't it be better to have the list ordered by the organizational chart, you know, so that the top dogs would be first on the list? So you sorted the list hierarchically.

---

59 You know she remembers everything. I know you do.

That's better.

Now you've moved the top execs, who are *Anna Recksiek, Dinah Soares, and Jacklyn Hyde,* to the top of the list.

	A	B	C
1	Team Members (Alphabetical)		Team Members (Hierarchical)
2	Anna Recksiek		Jacklyn Hyde
3	Bud Light		Anna Recksiek
4	Candy Kane		Dinah Soares
5	Chris P. Bacon		Constance Noring
6	Constance Noring		Don Key
7	Dinah Soares		Chris P. Bacon
8	Don Key		Bud Light
9	Eileen Dover		Pepe Roni
10	Jack Pott		Candy Kane
11	Jacklyn Hyde		Eileen Dover
12	Pepe Roni		Warren T.
13	Ty Coon		Jack Pott
14	Warren T.		Ty Coon

1 If your list is already entered into a sheet, select all of its elements. If it's not then start on step 2.

2 Click *File* tab ⇨ *Options* (way down) ⇨ *Advanced* (left pane, middle) ⇨ Scroll all the way down ⇨ *Edit Custom Lists* button. The *Custom Lists* dialog box opens up.

3 If you did step 1 then the range is already in the field *Import list from cells*, so just click *Import*. If not, you have two options. You can either Import it:
- Click inside the *Import* field.
- Select the range that holds the list.
- Click on the *Import* button.

Or create the list right there on the spot:

- Type it's elements either separated by commas or by *Enters* (which means one per row) into the right-hand side box.

- Click the *Add* button

Excel® displays the imported list on the left side, below the other lists she knows, as well as on the right side box.

4 Click *OK* to close the *Custom Lists* box.

5 Click *OK* to close the *Excel Options* box.

Now let's try it. Yeah, let's test your list.

1 Type any item in your list on any cell.

2 Pull The Thingy[60] to see how Excel® autofills it.

Notice that the list is now saved in the dialog box[61], so you'll be able to use it in any workbook in this computer. This also means that whenever you want to make changes (add

---

[60] The Thingy and how to pull it is discussed starting on page 81.

[61] It's actually saved in the computer's registry, but that's nerd talk. And frankly, who cares, as long as it works like the list of months, right?

elements, delete'em, or rearrange'em, you'll need to come to this dialog box and make the changes directly into the list.

Oops! (Warnings)

- *Custom Lists* can only contain *texts*. If you want a list of numbers you need to format them as text first.

- Keep in mind that for the Autofill feature to work properly you must type the seed-item *exactly* as it's saved in the list. Spelling matters. Capitals don't. If you like writing in capitals go ahead. I've written in DC, London, and Paris myself, and it's all been good.

Finally, Let's Use Our New List's Order to Sort a Second List of Related Data

Now that Excel® knows your list by heart, whenever *someone else* sends you a sheet that contains your coworkers' names in a *different order*, you can have Excel® sort them hierarchically, so that the new sheet will have them in the order that *you* want them to be. Isn't that fabulous?

As you probably already figured out, this feature (that allows you to sort data in the order established by a custom list) comes in incredibly handy when you want to sort data by the day of the week, because you really wouldn't want Excel® to do it alphabetically, and give you Fri, Mon, Sat, Sun, Thu, Tue, Wed, would you? Nope.

Same with months: if you had a list of transactions and one of the columns had the month in which they occurred as a text, you would probably prefer your list in the order Jan,

Feb, Mar, etc. rather than Apr, Aug, Dec, Feb, etc. (which is the alphabetical order.)

Example

Imagine you just got this list from the payroll dude (or dudette). Each row corresponds to an employee (or employette). The columns contain payroll data related to that person... you know, their ID, name, hourly wage, gross pay, hours worked... that kind 'a HR stuff.

	A	B	C	D	E	F		I	J	K	L	M
	Employee ID	Name	Hourly Wage	Hours	Gross Pay	Fe		Social Security 6.2%	Medicare 1.45%	Total Tax Withheld	Insurance Deduction	Net Pay
1												
2	2	Anna Recksiek	$10,607.50	10.00	$106,075.00			$6,576.65	$1,538.09	$44,079.37	$26.00	$61,969
3	7	Bud Light	$26.00	40.00	$1,040.00			$64.48	$15.08	$314.56	$35.00	$69
4	9	Candy Kane	$19.42	36.00	$699.12			$43.35	$10.14	$208.04	$26.00	$46
5	6	Chris P. Bacon	$28.12	39.00	$1,096.68			$67.99	$15.90	$355.90	$35.00	$705
6	4	Constance Noring	$34.00	40.00	$1,360.00			$84.32	$19.72	$447.84	$35.00	$877.
7	3	Dinah Soares	$9,788.00	15.00	$146,820.00			$9,102.84	$2,128.89	$61,031.93	$35.00	$85,753.07
8	5	Don Key	$34.00	42.00	$1,428.00			$88.54	$20.71	$440.69	$38.00	$949.31
9	10	Eileen Dover	$19.42	20.00	$388.40			$24.08	$5.63	$101.08	$26.00	$261.32
10	12	Jack Pott	$13.34	40.00	$533.60			$33.08	$7.74	$123.14	$36.00	$374
11	1	Jacklyn Hyde	$21,899.00	12.00	$262,788.00			$16,292.86	$3,810.43	$109,314.87	$37.00	$153,43
12	8	Pepe Roni	$21.15	45.00	$951.75			$59.01	$13.80	$195.01	$41.00	$71
13	13	Ty Coon	$12.89	43.00	$554.27			$34.36	$8.04	$96.51	$39.00	$41
			$16.97	36.00	$610.9					$171.31	$26.00	$4

If it wasn't that small and you could read it, you'd go, "Oh, sheet! The names are sorted alphabetically!" I know, right? No problemo. Let's sort them hierarchically.

1	Click on any cell in the data region (where data is, yeah, that's what a data region is.)
2	*Right click ⇨ Sort ⇨ Custom Sort.* Excel® automatically selects the whole region, and

3

recognizes that your range has headers. The *Sort* dialog box opens up.

Answer Excel®'s questions:

- *Column to sort by?* Pick Names.

- *Sort by Values, Cell Color, Font Color, or Cell Icon?* Pick *Values.*

- *Order A to Z, Z to A, or by Custom List...?* Pick *Custom List.* The Custom Lists dialog box pops up.

4

From the left side list, pick the one with the *Names* in the order we want them.

5

Click *OK* to close the *Custom List* dialog box.

6

Click *OK* to close the *Sort* dialog box.

Variations

- Instead of *Right clicking* on any cell, you could have *selected* the whole region and clicked on *Data tab* ⇨ *Sort* to open up the *Sort* dialog box (this would have replaced steps 1 and 2 in the above recipe.)

- If you get all the way into the *Custom List* dialog box and notice a list you thought was saved is not, you can create it right there on the spot.

- Actually, if it's a short list, it will be *faster* to just come to the *Custom Sort* and *Add* it here, rather than going through the lengthier process of entering it into a range, importing it to create a new list, and then coming to sort. Blagh.

- You can import more than one list at a time – just enter them as vertical lists in contiguous columns or as horizontal lists in contiguous rows, and select all of them before clicking on the *Import* button. Don't worry – Excel® is smart enough that to ask you whether the lists are vertical (by columns) or horizontal (by rows).

Secret #32. Autofill Sparklines

Sparklines, new in the 2010 version of Excel®, are tiny little charts that fit into one cell, come in three varieties (Line, Column, and Win-Loss), and can be autofilled. Some people think they're adorable, and some others think they're not a big deal. Let's see what *you* think of them.

Example

Last week you realized that you'd worked enough in your life, so it was time to invest in the stock market and make some easy money to retire in a month or so. Good thinking. You did some research, and picked five stocks to own; you bought a few shares of each one, and created a spreadsheet where you've been tracking their closing prices daily.

Analyzing trends and finding patterns is too much work when all you is a series of numbers. Then you remembered having heard *someone* say *something* like, "Isn't that what charts are for?" Oh, yeah. But charting takes time, and since you've worked enough in your life… how about creating sparklines instead? They're simple and fast. Sparklines, yes.

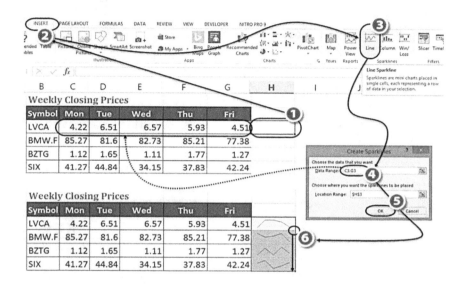

Creating Sparklines Method #1: Pulling The Thingy

1	Activate the first cell where you want the sparklines (G3).
2	On the Insert tab find the Sparklines group. Click on the type of Sparkline you want (Line).
3	In the dialog box, show Excel® where the data you want to chart is (B3:F3). This range should be in just one row or in just one column.

4	Click OK and enjoy your little Sparkline. Ahh.... Isn't that little cutie adorable?
5	Grab the Sparkline's cell's Thingy and pull it down to Autofill the rest. Double click won't work.
6	"Activate" any of them (click on it). By default Sparklines are treated as groups. Now the Sparkline Tools Tab is visible on your Ribbon. Its options allow you to change the Sparkline's color, add markers, change its type, etc.

Weekly Closing Prices

Symbol	Mon	Tue	Wed	Thu	Fri	Line	Column
LVCA	4.22	6.51	6.57	5.93	4.51		
BMW.F	85.27	81.6	82.73	85.21	77.38		
BZTG	1.12	1.65	1.11	1.77	1.27		
SIX	41.27	44.84	34.15	37.83	42.24		

Change from the Previous Day

Symbol	Mon	Tue	Wed	Thu	Fri	Win or Loss
LVCA		2.29	0.06	-0.64	-1.42	
BMW.F		-3.67	1.13	2.48	-7.83	
BZTG		0.53	-0.54	0.66	-0.5	
SIX		3.57	-10.69	3.68	4.41	

You can adapt the previous recipe to create a group of *Column* sparklines, and a group of *Win-Loss* ones[62].

---

[62] Caution: In *Column Sparklines* each row is drawn using a different scale, so don't compare column sizes from different rows.

Creating Sparklines Method #2: Using The Quick Analysis Tool

	A	B	C	D	E	F	G	H
1	Weekly Closing Prices							
2	Symbol	Mon	Tue	Wed	Thu	Fri		
3	LVCA	4.22	6.51	6.57	5.93	4.51		
4	BMW.F	85.27	81.6	82.73	85.21	77.38		
5	BZTG	1.12	1.65	1.11	1.77	1.27		
6	SIX	41.27	44.84	34.15	37.83	42.24		

FORMATTING   CHARTS   TOTALS   TABLES   SPARKLINES

Line   Win/Loss

Sparklines are mini charts placed in single cells.

	A	B	C	D	E	F	G
1	Weekly Closing Prices						
2	Symbol	Mon	Tue	Wed	Thu	Fri	
3	LVCA	4.22	6.51	6.57	5.93	4.51	
4	BMW.F	85.27	81.6	82.73	85.21	77.38	
5	BZTG	1.12	1.65	1.11	1.77	1.27	
6	SIX	41.27	44.84	34.15	37.83	42.24	

1   Select a range of data.

Win-Loss ones look too simple: their purpose is not to compare magnitudes, but just to show you which figures are negative (less than zero, not total downers.) To make finding the negatives easier, consider activating your Sparklines (click on any) and checking *Sparkline Tools Design* ⇨ *Negative Points* (in the *Show* group), so they'll be displayed in a different color.

2	The *Quick Analysis Button* appears near the bottom right corner of the selection. Click on it.
3	A gallery of options opens up. Click on *Sparklines.*
4	Pick the type of sparklines that you want: *Line, Column,* or *Win-Loss.* Excel creates a *Sparkline* for each row. Ta da!

Secret #33. How to use Flash Fill ("FiFi") to Split Texts

In Excel 2013 "the thingy" is on steroids. So much better than in previous versions! It's called *The Flash Fill* (*FF* or *FiFi* for short). This *FiFi*, is based on pattern recognition, and it's very powerful. Two common applications of this new feature are:

1. To have Excel® break texts into their components.
2. To change the case of text[63].

---

[63] Did you ever use the command *Data* ⇨ *Text to columns* to separate parts of strings of characters? Maybe you used text functions such as =LEFT(), =RIGHT(), =MID(), =FIND(), =LEN() etc. instead, right? How about =PROPER(), =UPPER(), or =LOWER() functions to change text to proper case, uppercase, or lowercase? No? Are you yawning? Oh, you were saying "Huh?"? Sorry. Anyway, never mind... whether you used commands and/or functions or spent half your life retyping data now you'll be amazed, because *Flash Fill* allows you to get the same results in an easier, faster, and more powerful way!

In this section we'll explore the first one.

Example

Let's start with a basic one. Let's have FiFi split full names into their components (first and last).

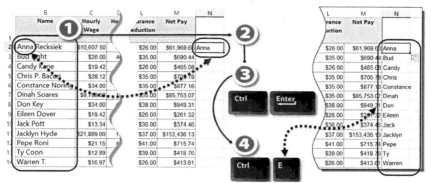

| | 1 | Type the full names you want to split as a vertical list (all in one column with no blank rows). |

| | 2 | Pick any column to the right of the list for the first names. It doesn't need to be immediately to the right of the full names. Type the first name for the first person in the list to show Excel® what part of the text you want. Wait! Don't press *Enter* yet! |

| | 3 | Press *Ctrl + Enter* instead, so that your cursor will stay on the first name instead of moving down to the cell below. |

| | 4 | Press *Ctrl + E*, which is the shortcut for the command *Data ⇨ Flash Fill*. Excel® fills the rest of the column with first names. As an alternative |

to using the shortcut you could have typed the second element in the resulting list (in this case the first name for the second person in your list) and Excel® suggests the rest.

More Examples

The following illustrations show you how FiFi can:

1. Split dates (take only the month, or only the year, for instance),

2. Split address into their components: number, street, city, etc.

In both examples I followed the steps listed above, which I'm repeating here in case you've already forgotten them (geez! Have you considered taking gingko biloba?)

Name	Address	Number	Street	City	State	Zip
Angelina Jolie	9336 Civic Center Drive, Beverly Hills, CA 90210	9336	Civic Center Drive	Beverly Hills	CA	90210
Halle Berry	1516 N. Fairfax Avenue, Los Angeles, CA 90046					
Bill Gates	1835 73rd Ave NE, Medina, WA 98039					
Tatum Channing	9111 Wilshire Blvd., Beverly Hills, CA 90210					
Santa Claus	101 St. Nicholas Drive North Pole, AK 99705					
Shakira	1411 Broadway 39th Floor, New York, NY 10018					

Name	Address	Number	Street	City	State	Zip
Angelina Jolie	9336 Civic Center Drive, Beverly Hills, CA 90210	9336	Civic Center Drive	Beverly Hills	CA	90210
Halle Berry	1516 N. Fairfax Avenue, Los Angeles, CA 90046	1516	N. Fairfax Avenue	Los Angeles	CA	90046
Bill Gates	1835 73rd Ave NE, Medina, WA 98039	1835	Ave NE	Medina	WA	98039
Tatum Channing	9111 Wilshire Blvd., Beverly Hills, CA 90210	9111	Wilshire Blvd.	Beverly Hills	CA	90210
Santa Claus	101 St. Nicholas Drive North Pole, AK 99705	101	St. Nicholas Drive North	AK 99705	AK	99705
Shakira	1411 Broadway 39th Floor, New York, NY 10018	1411	Broadway 39th Floor	New York	NY	10018

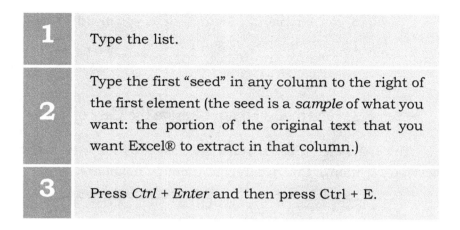

1   Type the list.

2   Type the first "seed" in any column to the right of the first element (the seed is a *sample* of what you want: the portion of the original text that you want Excel® to extract in that column.)

3   Press *Ctrl + Enter* and then press Ctrl + E.

Considerations

- You have to be careful with FiFi. Use FiFi to *Flash Fill* one column at a time (for instance you can't enter the first first-name and the first last-name, select them both and then press *Ctrl + E* to autofill both columns down. Won't work. You have to do one column at a time... had I already said that? Oops).

- Always confirm the results (some patterns may be ambiguous, some data may have a slightly different format, some data may be inconsistent, etc.) because, like any other female, Excel®'s not always perfect. For instance, take Santa's address in the second example above and notice how it was not well split because there was a comma missing between the street and the city.

- FiFi is not a function. It replaces functions, but it's not one of them. This means that it will not recalculate, so when you change the source data you need to have FiFi perform its magic again.

Secret #34. How to use FiFi to Change the Case of Text

The steps are quite the same ones that you followed in the previous section... Can you repeat them by memory?

Mixed Case Names	Proper Case Names		Mixed Case Names	Proper Case Names
anna recksiek	Anna Recksiek		anna recksiek	Anna Recksiek
BUD LIGHT			BUD LIGHT	Bud Light
CANDY KANE			CANDY KANE	Candy Kane
CHRIS P. BACON			CHRIS P. BACON	Chris P. Bacon
constance noring			constance noring	Constance Noring
dinah soares			dinah soares	Dinah Soares
don key			don key	Don Key
EILEEN DOVER			EILEEN DOVER	Eileen Dover
jack pott			jack pott	Jack Pott
jacklyn hyde			jacklyn hyde	Jacklyn Hyde
PEPE RONI			PEPE RONI	Pepe Roni
ty coon			ty coon	Ty Coon
WARREN T.			WARREN T.	Warren T.

1	Type the list.
2	Type the first "seed" in any column to the right of the first element (the seed is a *sample* of what you want: in this case it's the original text in upper, lower, or proper case).
3	Press *Ctrl + Enter*.
4	Press *Ctrl + E*.

Best Places to Double Click[64]

Secret #35. On Any Dialog Box to Skip the OK

The title says it all, doesn't it? Double click on your selection instead of clicking on it and then clicking on the OK button whenever you are making a selection on a dialog box (except for check boxes and drop-down lists).

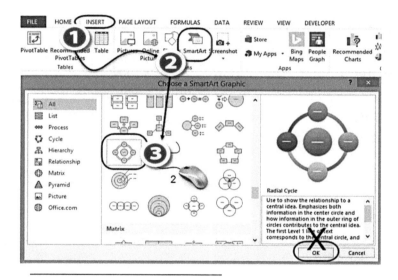

---

[64] Double clicking on *The Thingy* is Secret #25.

Double-clicking on any number in a pivot table (called "drilling down") will be covered in volume 2. If you can't wait I can tell you that when you double click on a number Excel® creates a table (in a new sheet) that shows you the details of where it came from. For instance, if the number you double clicked on is Petunia's total sales, the table that Excel® creates will list every transaction she has closed that was included when calculating the total figure you double clicked on.

Secret #36. A Ribbon Tab's Edge

Double clicking any of the Ribbon tab's edges toggles between viewing an open and a closed ribbon[65].

When you want more area to work on your sheet, close the Ribbon. You won't lose anything, because whenever you need a command, you can just click on a tab and it will open up the Ribbon back.

This shortcut is the same as clicking on the *Ribbon Display Options* icon to the right of the *Help* icon, on the top right of your Excel® window, right above the Ribbon. The options are self-explanatory[66].

? ⊞ — 🗗 ✕

Auto-hide Ribbon
Hide the Ribbon. Click at the top of the application to show it.

Show Tabs
Show Ribbon tabs only. Click a tab to show the commands.

Show Tabs and Commands
Show Ribbon tabs and commands all the time.

Do *not* hide your coworkers' ribbon. It's not nice.

---

[65] Some people call it an *expanded* or a *collapsed* ribbon. Those are big words for me though.

[66] You may have noticed (in the illustration above) the diamonds to the left of the help icon (question mark). Now that you know Excel is female, and since "diamonds are girls' best friends," you may want to give your Excel some too. Wait! Before rushing to the jeweler, try this: Click on *File* ⇨ *Options* ⇨ *General*, and under the *Personalize your copy of Microsoft Office* group of options, right below your User name, pick *Doodle Diamonds* as the *Office Background*. Try other options, such as Clouds, Stars, Underwater, etc. just to add variety every now and then. Who said nerds don't know how to be adventurous? Ha.

Secret #37. A Row's or a Column's Edge

Double click on a **column's** right edge (or on a **row's** bottom edge) to tell Excel® to adjust the column's width (or the row's height) to accommodate the widest (or tallest) data in that column (or row). This is referred to as *Autofit*.

You may have noticed that when you hover over any column's or row's edge, the pointer's shape changes to a black cross with a double-headed arrow in the direction in which Excel® will expand or contract if you click and drag.

Example

- You've entered into column *A* a list of cities in Alabama[67] that you're considering relocating to. Hover the cursor over the right edge of column A, and when it looks as described above, double click. Now column A is wide enough. To widen several columns at the same time just select all of them first, and when all of their letters are highlighted, double click on the right edge of the rightmost column. Ta da!

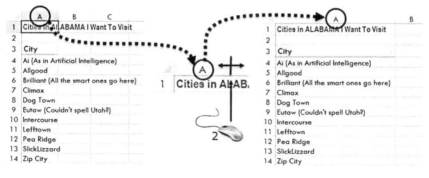

---

[67] Tersigni (2008).

Secret #38. A Sheet Tab

To change a worksheet's name, double click on its name tab and type the new one (same as *Right click ⇨ Rename.*)

Secret #39. The Format Painter Tool

Have you ever used the *Format Painter* to copy the formatting from one range to another? Perhaps you didn't know its technical name —I'm talking about the little brush you can find in several places, such as the two illustrated here:

(1) *Home* tab ⇨ *Clipboard* group, and

(2) The mini toolbar that pops up when you *right click* on a cell or range.

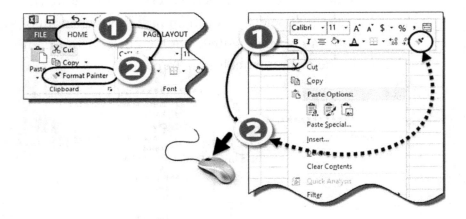

This is how it's used:

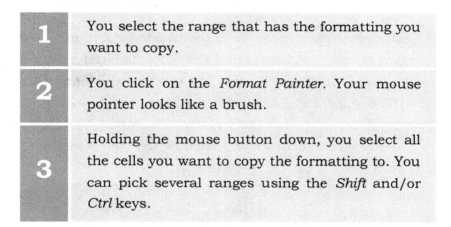

1	You select the range that has the formatting you want to copy.
2	You click on the *Format Painter*. Your mouse pointer looks like a brush.
3	Holding the mouse button down, you select all the cells you want to copy the formatting to. You can pick several ranges using the *Shift* and/or *Ctrl* keys.

When you let go of the mouse button your cursor goes back to normal —the tool is gone. That means that if you want to copy the same formatting to other range(s) (perhaps you missed them, or hadn't thought about it) you need to pick up the tool again first, unless... ... You double click on it!

If you pick it up with a double instead of a single click, the tool will remain active until you click on its icon again, or press *Esc*.

By the way, did you know that you can use the format painter to copy the formatting from one object to another? Yes, you can. For instance, if you have a rectangle that you've formatted with certain fill color and a certain type of border and border color, and you want to copy that formatting to a star you've drawn in your sheet, you can use the *Format Painter* as you would with cells.

Secret #40. The Autosum Icon

Who doesn't love to use the *Autosum* command to calculate totals? You know, that Greek sigma letter icon that some people call "The sideways M" and that you find in the *Home* Tab ⇨ *Editing* group, or in the *Formula* tab ⇨ *Function Library* group, or in your *Quick Access Toolbar*[68].

I've seen a lot of convoluted "techniques," but it's better to just KISS (Keep It Simple Sweetheart):

1	Click on the cell where you want the total.
2	Double click on the *Autosum* icon.

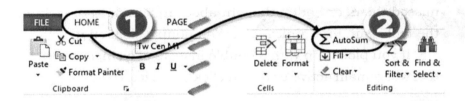

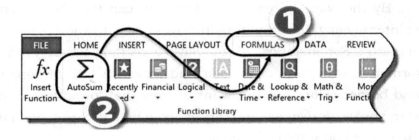

---

[68] If you use it a lot you've got to have it in your *Quick Access Toolbar*. To learn how to place it there read Secret #6.

Double clicking instead of clicking and pressing (or clicking) *Enter* works *only* with *simple* Autosums. By *simple* I mean that you're summing the range immediately above or to the left of the total, so Excel® can guess that range correctly.

Otherwise —if the cells to sum are all over, or there are intermediate blank cells, for instance— then the double click won't help you: you'll have to total "the traditional way": clicking on the *Autosum* icon, then entering (or pointing at) the range to sum, and then hitting *Enter*.

Secret #41. A Formula

You can edit a formula directly inside the cell where it is, instead of on the formula bar[69]. Just double click on it. When editing a formula on-site the mouse pointer looks like a pipe (vertical line), Excel® color codes the cells used in the formula and their addresses, and the navigation and editing keys[70] move the cursor inside the cell.

	A	B
1	Sales	120
2	Cost of goods sold	65
3	Gross profit	=B1-B2

Some of you are thinking, "Isn't that the same as F2?" Absolutely! You can also edit a cell on-site by selecting it and pressing F2, but I must warn you: F2 is so totally 80s! If you want to look and feel younger you'd better drop the F2 and start double clicking[71].

If instead of double clicking on a cell you double click the black square on its bottom right corner (a.k.a. "The Thingy"), then you'll be autofilling the formula down. Excel® will automatically update the relative references in the formula so they'll point at the appropriate cells.

---

[69] To edit a formula in the formula bar (1) click on the cell that contains the formula, (2) click on the formula bar and edit it there.

[70] Left arrow, right arrow, delete, backspace, home and end.

[71] What if you don't have a mouse? Oh. Well. In that case use F2, but please do it discretely.

Secret #42. A Chart[72]

When you double click on any element of a chart (such as its title, vertical axis, legend, grid, labels, etc.) Excel® opens a pane on the right side of your window to display all your options to format that specific element.

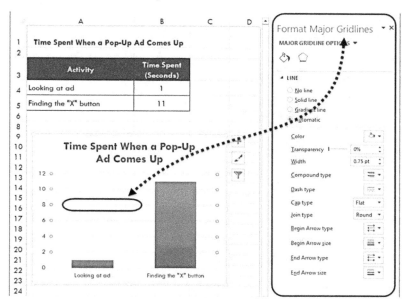

Since this pane doesn't interfere with other areas of your window, you may as well leave it open until you're done formatting all parts of your chart. The fact that it stays open until you specifically close it means that you can go back and forth between the formatting pane and the chart itself, and whenever you select a different part of the chart, Excel® automatically updates the formatting menu to offer you the

---

[72] Funny charts courtesy of Graphjam.com (2014).

options applicable to the part of the chart selected.

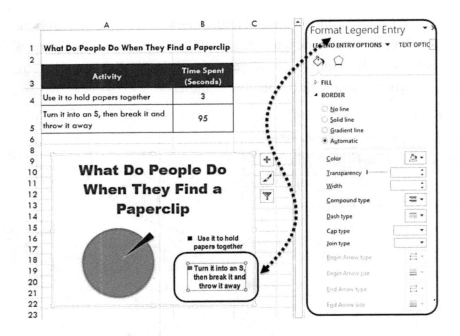

Secret #43. On a Cell's Border

Click on the top/right/down/left border of any cell to move fast to the top/right/down/left. Double clicking on that cell's border is like pressing *Ctrl* and the arrow in the direction you want to move: it takes you to the last cell occupied in that block of contiguous cells (a.k.a. region).

For other techniques to move fast see Secret #50. Here are a couple examples[73]:

---

[73] 247Wallst.com (2014).

The Most Powerful Keyboard Shortcuts

Secret #44. How to Execute Any Command with Your Keyboard

1   Press the *Alt key* (look for it to the left of the space bar.) Excel® displays a *Keytip* (letter or number) associated with each *Ribbon Tab,* and one *Keytip* next to each tool in the *QAT.*

2	Press the *Keytip* that corresponds to the *tab* (or tool) you want to select. If you selected a Ribbon Tab, Excel® shows you a *Keytip* for each of its commands. Press the Keytip that corresponds to the command, task, or gallery that you want.
3	Keep going for as many levels as needed, following the path of *Keytips* that Excel® displays to guide you. Follow the next illustrated example.

Note: If the command you want is neither in *The Ribbon* nor in the *Quick Access Toolbar* (*QAT*) place it there first. See Secret #6.

Example

To give cell C1 a *Title* formatting (using the *Title* predefined formatting style) activate that cell (by clicking on it) and press *Alt* ⇨ *H* ⇨ *J* ⇨ *Down arrow* three times ⇨ *Right arrow* four times ⇨ *Enter.*

Those movements allow you to select the desired predefined style before you press *Enter* to choose it.

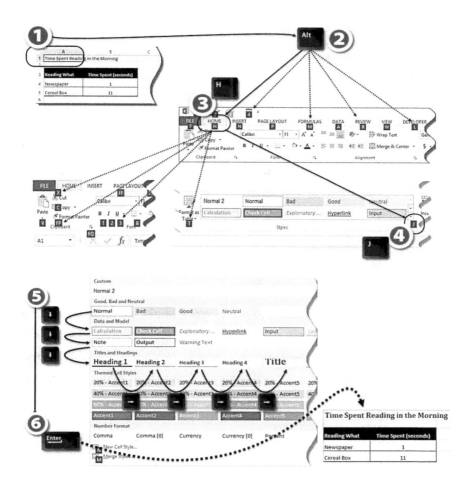

Save Tons of Time When Formatting

I know this is not a keyboard shortcut, but since the example above had you use *predefined formatting styles*, I thought we might as well include them here, don't you think? (No need to answer, thanks anyway.)

Bear with me. You'll like them. The predefined styles in the gallery allow you to format way faster than applying individual formatting features to your cells (bold, center, font color, fill color, etc.) over and over.

A few more things you need to know to get started with predefined styles:

- You can modify them. Right click ⇨ *Modify*.

- You can also create your own *Custom Styles*. Select *Home* ⇨ *Cell Styles* ⇨ *New Style*. Give it a one-word not-previously-used name. Now pick all the features you want to assign to your new style. *Custom* styles are shown in the gallery at the top.

- To create a new style you can also format any cell the way you want it, select it, and then click on *Home* ⇨ *Cell Styles* ⇨ *New Style*.

- Styles are unique to each workbook, so if you want to "bring over" to a new book the styles you previously created in another) use *Home* ⇨ *Cell Styles* ⇨ *Merge Styles*. If you used colors from the original book's palette and the new book has a different one, your styles will be adapted accordingly when you merge them.

Thanks for letting me digress. Now let's go back to our keyboard shortcuts, shall we?

Secret #45. Don't Lose Ctrl + 1

How to Open the Format Dialog Box

When you select a cell (or cells), shape, chart, or any other object[74] and then press *Ctrl + 1*, Excel opens up a *Format* dialog box with formatting options for that specific type of object.

The following illustrations[75] show three different *Format* dialog boxes (*Format Chart Area, Format Picture,* and *Format Text)* that are displayed when pressing *Ctrl + 1* on a chart, on a picture, or on your nose. Ha. Just checking if you're still awake.

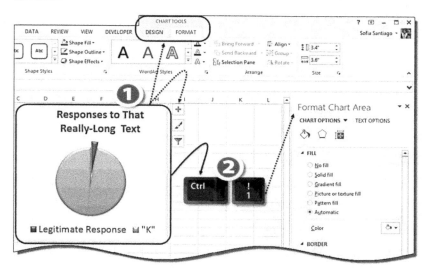

---

[74] The element you selected is the "active" element. The "active something" is not the "something" that likes skiing or dances Zumba... it is just the one that is selected at the time.

[75] Funny charts courtesy of Graphjam.com (2014).

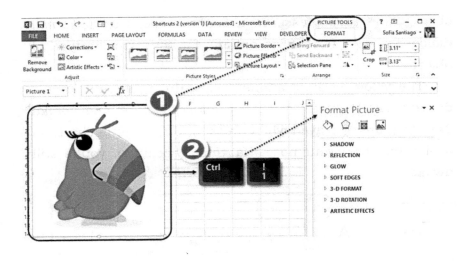

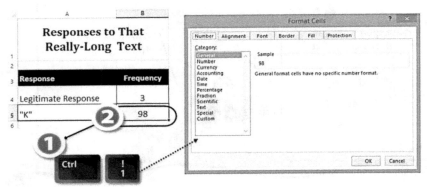

There are other ways to open up the *Format* dialog box specific for the active object:

- Right click and select Format <object selected>.

- For cells click on the small arrow to the right of the group names in the *Home* tab, as shown next.

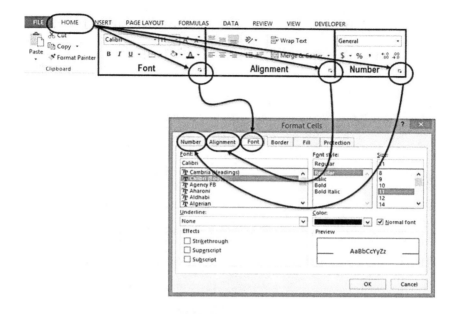

Secret #46. Ctrl + Mustache

Ctrl + Mustache is the shortcut for the command *View* ➪ *Formulas.*

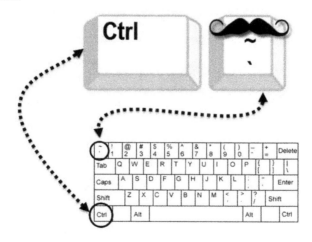

1 Find the *Mustache* key in your keyboard. It's a key that has the *tilde* character (~) and the *French accent* or *grave accent* (`) below it. It's usually to the left of the number one.

2 Press the *Ctrl* key, and hold it down while you press the *Mustache* key. Look at your sheet and you'll see the formulas instead of their results.

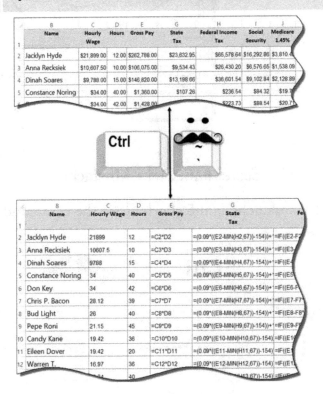

When you press this key combination over and over the view alternates between values and formulas. Values. *Ctrl + Mustache*. Formulas. *Ctrl + Mustache*. Values. Ad infinitum.

Warning: don't fret if when you press *Ctrl + Mustache* for the first time the dollar symbols and other formatting vanishes. It's okay. It will come back when you press *Ctrl + Mustache* again.

Those who don't know that Excel® stores dates as numbers[76] may feel uneasy when they see their dates all stripped out of their date formatting. It's like seeing your girlfriend without makeup for the first time. May be scary, but when you make a conscious effort to remind yourself that her "content" hasn't changed, and that when she puts her makeup on again it will all be all right, you can calm down. After all, what is formatting but makeup for cells, right?

So did you like this Shortcut? Will you use it? And don't you think that *Ctrl Mustache* sounds more friendly (and easier to remember) than *Ctrl + grave accent*? Me too.

---

[76] 1/1/1900 is day 1, 1/2/1900 is day 2 ... 8/6/2014 is day 41857, 8/7/2014 is 41858, etc. Excel® stores dates this way to make "date math" easy. For instance, if on cell A1 you enter the date 1/1/2015, and on cell A2 you enter the formula =A1+7, then cell A2 will display 1/8/2015, which is seven days added to the first date. If now you grab cell's A2's Thingy (bottom right corner) and pull it down, you'll be filling column A with a list of dates that are each seven days after the previous one (a list of Mondays, for instance).

Here's another example: to calculate the number of days between two dates, just type a formula that subtracts the cell that contains one of them from the cell that contains the other, as in =B2-B4, where B2 and B4 are both dates. Capish? Capish.

Secret #47. How to Split the Text Inside One Cell Into Two or More Lines

Wrapping Text

When the text inside a cell is too wide, but you don't want to widen the column, or to see it spilling over the next cell, you can *Wrap* it: Excel® splits it into several lines within one cell.

Alt + Enter

Instead of the *Wrap Text* command (which is in the *Home* Tab, *Alignment* group) you can "manually" insert an *Alt + Enter* to tell Excel® *exactly* where you want her to split the text. She then considers this text "Wrapped." Here's an example:

- Select any cell

- Type I am

- Press Alt + Enter

- Type TOTALLY,

- Press Alt + Enter

- Type Awesome

- Press Enter

  Smile big and think "Oh yeah, baby"

Do you see how handy this Shortcut will be next time you want to split a long heading into two lines within the same cell? Me too.

Oh, by the way, you can combine the *Wrap Text* command with the *Merge and Center* command to split a long text into several lines while at the same time having it centered over several columns. You can issue the two commands in any order, but you may need to adjust the row height afterwards to show all lines.

Here's an example. Look at the title in the illustration on page 8 (The Five Highest-Paying Jobs You Can Get with a High School Degree.) Here are the three commands from the *Alignment* group (*Home* tab) I used:

- I entered the text into cell A1

- I selected cells A1 and B1

- I clicked on *Home* ⇨ *Wrap Text*

- I clicked on Home ⇨ Merge and Center

- I clicked on *Home* ⇨ *Middle Align*

Secret #48. Cloning Sheets Without Even Right Clicking!

Whenever you want to create a copy of a worksheet in *the same* workbook, do this:

1	Click on the name tab of the sheet you want to duplicate.
2	Hold down the *Ctrl* key and keep it down until we're done.
3	Do what you would if you were going to move this sheet to change its order within the list of worksheets in this book: grab the sheet's name (by clicking on it) and drag and drop it in the location on the sheet's-names-list where you want the clone. Excel® gives the new sheet the same name as the original followed by a (2), (3), etc. depending on how many clones you've created.
4	Double click the clone's name to rename it[77].

If you want to move or copy it into another workbook use *Move or Copy Sheet*:

---

[77] This command is not undoable.

1	Open both workbooks (source and destination).
2	Find the sheet you want to copy and right click on its name tab.
3	Select *Move* or *Copy*.
4	Tell Excel® • Which workbook to copy it to • Before which sheet you want it, or if you want it to be the last sheet there.
5	Check the *Create a copy* box.
6	Click *OK*.

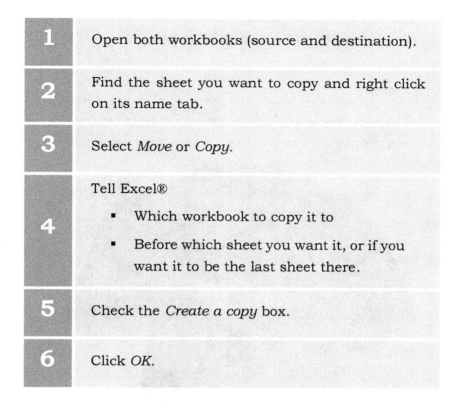
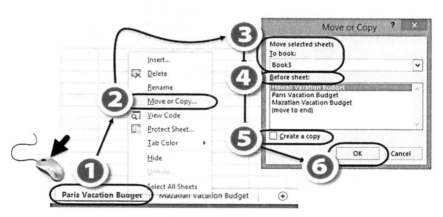

Secret #49. Shift Happens®

Shift + Move

When you *move* a cell[78] you're not actually moving the cell (as a container)... What you're moving is the cell's contents. In

---

[78] If you haven't done it before (moving a cell, yes) try it now: click on the cell you want to move and hover your cursor over its frame. When the mouse pointer turns into a four headed arrow, click, and holding down the mouse click, move the mouse to the new location where you want to "drop" the data. Once you're over that new location release the mouse button. The old cell is empty and the data has moved to the new location. If you "drop" the data into a cell that's already

contrast, when you hold down *Shift* while moving a cell (or cells), it seems as if you're actually moving the physical cell(s). When you hold *Shift* while moving, Excel® inserts the cell(s) you're moving into the new location *and* removes it (them) from the old location, so you don't have to!

If you *Shift + Move* a cell and try to drop it on top of another cell that has data, it will not replace that data— instead, Excel® will insert the moved-cell, pushing down any other cells in the destination location as necessary to make room for the data that's being moved.

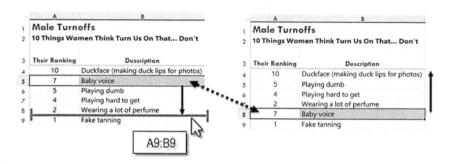

Example

So you found a list of things women think turn men on that...don't. You copied the ones not rated R into a spreadsheet[79]. Before giving copies to everyone you want to sort them in a different order. You want to move row 5 (Baby voice) just above fake tanning.

occupied with data, Excel® asks you if you want to replace the contents of the destination cell.

[79] Askmen.com (2014).

1	Select the cell(s) you want to *Shift + Move* (in this case A5:B5). You can select a whole row.
2	Holding down *Shift*, hover your mouse over the frame that surrounds the selection until your cursor looks like a four headed black arrow. Click, hold, and move them down (by sliding your mouse) until the gray horizontal line that Excel® displays to guide you is where you want the cells to be now (in this case it's between rows 8 and 19 and the tip reads A9:B9 (these cells will be the data's new addresses.)
3	Let go. Notice how Excel® *shifts* all the cells up to fill the gap that moving the-cells-we-moved (in this case row 5) left.

Secret #50. Moving in a New York Minute

Move from One Sheet to Another like Nobody's Business

So you already knew that the arrows to the left of your list of sheet names[80] allow you to move from one sheet to another, right? And you know that you can use the three vertical dots to their right to make more room for the sheet names. Okay.

---

[80] Above the mode indicator (in the bottom left corner of your window, above the status bar).

But... are you still click-click-click-click-clicking on the arrows until you find the sheet you want? Be honest. Are you?

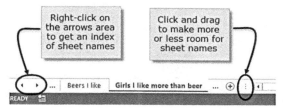

If so, you'll love this shortcut: Right click on the arrows. Excel® will display a list of the sheets in this workbook that you can use as an index. Click on any and you'll get there. The last item in the list, if you have more than can fit, reads *More Sheets...* If you click on it Excel® displays a dialog box for you to pick the sheet you want to go to.

Other Ways to Move Really Fast

I've seen even the most experienced users move through lists with hundreds of rows using their mouse wheel like tic, tic, tic, tic, tic.... As fast as they can...moving their middle finger like the tiny legs of a hamster on steroids in an exercise wheel. You get the picture. No excuse: from now on you must practice these shortcuts *constantly*.

Key/ Key combination	Move ...
PgDn or PgUp	One screen down / up
Alt + PgDn or Alt + PgUp	One screen right/left

Ctrl + Arrow Keys	To edge of next data region
Home	To beginning of a row
Ctrl + Home	To beginning of worksheet
Ctrl + End	To the last cell (bottom right corner) that has content (or had content and it has been deleted) since last Save
Ctrl + f	Displays Find & Replace
Shift + F4	Repeat last find

Start, for instance, with *Ctrl* key and the arrow in the direction in which you want to move. Try it, so you'll see how

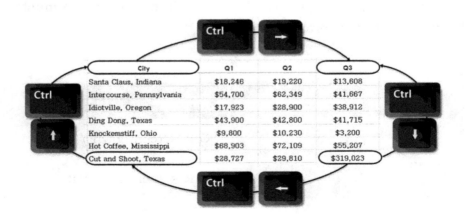

it works, and where that key combination takes you depending on where you are when you press it.

If you are on a cell that's part of a region (which is a group of contiguous cells that are populated with data[81]) *Ctrl + Arrow* will take you to the last cell of the current region in the direction of the arrow.

If you are already on the last cell of a region it will take you to the first cell of the next region, or if there is no other region in that direction, it will take you to the end of the world (or the end of Excel®'s sheet, whichever occurs first).

You can accomplish the same result by double-clicking on the border of a cell (see Secret #43.)

Going Directly to Any Cell

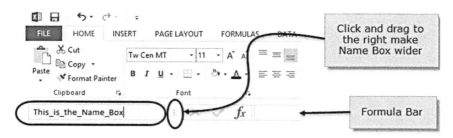

You can type a cell reference directly into the *Name Box*, and that will take you directly to that cell. This is like typing a reference (cell address, like A34, or W99) using *Home ⇨ Find & Select ⇨ Go to* (in the *Editing* group).

Bon voyage!

---

[81] Yeah, I know... I may have said it before, but I didn't take my gingko biloba memory supplement today...

Epilogue

In 2013 Forbes published an article titled *Microsoft's Excel Might Be the Most Dangerous Software on the Planet*[82]. Of course I had to read it! It starts like this:

> *No, really, it's possible that Microsoft's Excel is the most dangerous software on the planet. Yes, more dangerous than rogue code running a nuclear power plant, than the Stuxnet that was deliberately sent off to sabotage Iran's nuclear program, worse, even, than whatever rent in the fabric of space time led to the invention of Lolcats. Really, that serious.*

Did you understand that? I didn't. I didn't know that space time paid rent, or that a cat that laughs was called a Lolcat (if indeed I guessed right and that's what a Lolcat is.) So I did what I do when I read something that I don't understand. I skipped that sentence and kept reading.

> *There's a danger at one level: it's all become so complex and it's handled in such a slapdash manner that no one is really on top of it anymore.*

Okay, that I get. I thought I was on top of Excel® though. Anyway, the article then explains how JP Morgan was "running huge bets" (tens of *billions* of dollars,) and checking what they were doing "playing around in Excel." Long story short, these guys were cutting and pasting from one

---

[82] Forbes (2013).

spreadsheet to another, and they got one of the equations wrong, which resulted in the bank losing *several billion dollars.*

Can you believe that? Basic cutting and pasting. Several *billion* dollars. Holly cow. That's *a bit* more than what I'll make in my whole lifetime, working like a dog. How about you?

Now, who do you think paid for that? The stockholders? Their clients? The markets? Do you think that all kinds of people from all over world might have felt the butterfly effect of these people's carelessness?

Do you think it's okay to blame a wonderful tool for our carelessness using it?

I don't.

That's why what you're doing is huge.

Congratulations on having bought this book (my retirement account congratulates you too.) But most importantly, for *investing* your time and energy in reading it, learning, and improving yourself. I'm convinced that it will not only benefit *you* tremendously, but it will impact many more people than you might ever know.

As for me? Well, I love Excel®. And the same way I know that in some hands she can really be dangerous, I know that in competent and ethical hands she can be a blessing. Excel® gives us back *our time.* And our time is one of our most valuable possessions, isn't it?

So remember: Shift happens™. Stay in Ctrl™.

Sofia Santiago

Acknowledgments

Thanks to:

- All the authors of the works cited.

- My friend Rick Beemer, for being a sounding board, and for handcuffing me to the typewriter until I finished.

- My daughter Dani De la Chica, for designing the preliminary cover, interior, and website.

- My mum. Thanks to her I wrote this book in twelve months. I could have written it in two though. Mom, I don't even want to think what I'd do without you.

- The thousands of people who have attended my seminars, because their laughs and enthusiastically positive evaluations encouraged me to undertake this project. Special thanks to those who cried. Of joy.

- Finally, thanks to Excel®. If you didn't exist, less people would read this book (I guess), so thanks.

Works Cited

247Wallst.com (2014). *The 15 Highest-Paying Companies in America*. Retrieved on 9/1/14 from http://247wallst.com/special-report/2014/03/18/the-15-highest-paying-companies-in-america/print/

Abrahams, Marlon (2014). *Big Bum, Bright Babies*. Retrieved from http://www.parent24.com/Getting_pregnant/Big-bum-bright-babies-20090824 on 6/1/14.

AOL (2011). *$100,000 Jobs You Can Get With A High School Degree*. Retrieved on 7/1/14 from http://jobs.aol.com/articles/2011/08/15/the-highest-paying-jobs-you-can-get-with-a-high-school-degree/

Askmen.com (2014). Male *Turnoffs: 10 things women think turn men on that...don't*. Retrieved from http://www.askmen.com/top_10/dating/male-turn-offs.html

Forbes (2013). *Microsoft's Excel Might Be The Most Dangerous Software On The Planet*. Retrieved on 1/6/2016 from http://www.forbes.com/sites/timworstall/2013/02/13/microsofts-excel-might-be-the-most-dangerous-software-on-the-planet/

Graphjam.com (2014). Charts retrieved on 2/2/2014 from http://izismile.com/2010/02/03/funny_statistics_43_pics.html

Murano, Grace (2009). *15 Funniest Street and Roads Names*. Retrieved on 2/2/14 from http://www.oddee.com/item_96898.aspx

Phalange, Regina (2013). *Awesome Uses for Big Booties.* Use #23. Retrieved on 2/12/2014 from http://www.rantchic.com/2013/12/04/awesome-uses-for-big-booties/?utm_medium= referral&utm_source=Taboola&utm_term=Title1

Soniak, Matt and De Main, Bill (2014). *15 Places With Strange Names and How They Got Them.* Mentalfloss. Retrieved on 9/21/14 from http://mentalfloss.com/article/27987/15-places-strange-names-and-how-they-got-them

Squidoo (2014). *Strange Street Names.* Retrieved on 2/2/14 from http://www.squidoo.com/ strange_street_names#module147821697

Tersigni, Dean (2008). *Unusual City Names.* Retrieved on 2/2/14 from http://www. thealmightyguru.com/Pointless/Cities.html

Zak, Paul (2012). *TEDx Amsterdam Women: Paul Zak - The Differences Between Men and Women,* retrieved on 10/10/14 from https://www.youtube.com /watch?v=Sm0xPCyRWNA#t=712